New Ways in Teacher Education

Donald Freeman, with Steve Cornwell, Editors

New Ways in TESOL Series
Innovative Classroom Techniques
Jack C. Richards, Series Editor
Teachers of English to Speakers of Other Languages, Inc.

Typeset in Garamond Book and Tiffany Demi
by Automated Graphic Systems, White Plains, Maryland, USA
and printed by Pantagraph Printing, Bloomington, Illinois USA

Teachers of English to Speakers of Other Languages, Inc.
700 South Washington Street, Suite 200
Alexandria, Virginia 22314 USA
Tel 703-836-0774 • Fax 703-836-7864 • E-mail tesol@tesol.org • http//www.tesol.org/

Director of Communications and Marketing: Helen Kornblum
Senior Editor: Marilyn Kupetz
Spot Art: Ann Kammerer
Cover Design: Capitol Communications Systems, Inc., Crofton, Maryland, USA
Illustrations: David Connell

ISBN 0-939791-46-3
LOC 94-060126

To Earl Stevick,

*whose work has shaped for many of us
how we think about teaching and learning
and what we do in our classrooms*

Contents

Acknowledgments

I would like to thank the following people for their involvement in this project, which has truly been a collective effort: Jack Richards, who suggested the project in the first place; Susan Keil and Cynthia Stinson, who helped enter various revisions in the manuscript; Mary Scholl, who created an elegant index that brought order and accessibility to the content; Steve Cornwell, who signed on at the very beginning of the project and quickly came to be its heart and soul, the person without whose common sense and good humor the book never would have been completed; the Master of Arts in Teaching Program at the School for International Training, which provided ongoing logistical support to the project; Helen Kornblum and Marilyn Kupetz in the TESOL Central Office, who brought this book out with care and professionalism; and TESOL colleagues around the world, whose shared experience, expertise, and insights into how people learn to teach second languages make up this volume.

Introduction

When I was first asked to put together this book on "new ways" in teacher education, I thought—perhaps naively—that it would be a straightforward task. As part of a series that focuses on how to do things in classrooms, the book would need to concentrate on activities, as opposed to theoretical or programmatic accounts, in teacher education. Beyond that initial direction, however, the framing of the book has involved a lot of give-and-take and has in fact developed as a sort of ongoing conversation. Several topics in that conversation are worth mentioning in this introduction for two reasons: They capture current, critical issues in second language teacher education and they help to make clear how the book is put together.

Defining the Content

The first turn in the conversation had to do with content. Was this to be a book about how to teach language or how to teach teachers? For some who wrote, these two processes seemed to be one and the same. We received contributions from second language classrooms that colleagues found valuable and therefore wanted to suggest as useful for other teachers. From this perspective, a teacher education book would contain techniques and activities for learning language and would introduce teaching by presenting the tried-and-true practices of classroom teachers. Other writers sent activities they use with people who are learning how to teach in order to help them understand effective classroom practice. From this perspective, the book would contain activities that helped people grasp what teaching is and how to do it. It would introduce teaching by presenting activities through which people could develop their own independent, reflective practice as classroom teachers.

This basic difference over what teacher education should involve is an illuminating one. Is learning to teach a matter of replicating how other teachers do things? Or does it depend on coming to grips with one's own ways of thinking and doing things in the classroom? In this book, we take the position that learning to teach is a process that, while it can be informed by the knowledge and insight of others, remains principally the responsibility and work of the learner.

This book contains 46 different activities that teacher educators in various contexts around the world use in helping people learn to teach. As such, some of the activities are specific to learning how to teach second languages, but most can be considered generic in that they can address the learning of teaching of any subject matter. All share an emphasis on what the learners-of-teaching bring to—and what they do in—the process of becoming independent, self-sufficient classroom practitioners.

Defining the Learner

A second turn in the conversation had to do with the learner. Although the book is addressed to teacher educators, the question arose: To which learners-of-teaching is this book directed? There is certainly no shortage of distinctions one can make among learners-of-teaching: preservice trainees, in-service teachers, graduate students in MA programs, practicing teachers, novice or experienced practitioners, native or nonnative English-speaking teachers, and so on. These distinctions make us attend to the various contexts in which teaching is learned. They also call attention to the fact that teaching is learned over time, so it is useful to differentiate among learners at various points in their development. As we are understanding from research in teacher cognition, teachers in different stages of their careers benefit from different ways of learning to teach.

We have chosen not to focus on differences in context, experience, or background, but to suggest these factors through the narratives introducing each contribution. We have included a cross-section of activities that address different contexts, phases in learning to teach, and phases that span the processes of teacher training and teacher development. Although some activities will be suited to particular situations, the majority can be used in or adapted to different settings and groups of learners-of-teaching. The Users' Guide to Activities immediately following this introduction clusters the activities according to various criteria. It is meant to provide a way into the wealth and variety of know-how in the book and to suggest the multiple ways in which the activities can be used.

Defining the Approach

Underlying the preceding two exchanges is the fundamental issue in the book, namely how teaching is learned. There are clearly diverse views represented here, for this is a conversation among practitioners of teacher education. However, to simply call the variety *diverse views* obscures a common core. All the contributions share, to one degree or another, an orientation that comes not from selective editing, but from what emerges as a common perspective. What qualifies these activities as "new" ways in teacher education is their emphasis on how teachers—like any learners—come to make sense of what they do.

The contributors to this book are responding, in some basic way, to the imprint of the knowledge-transmission model of education. They resist the assumption that people will learn to teach just by being told what to do or how to do it. Just as students must build their own understandings of a second language in order to use it well, so too must learners-of-teaching construct a view of the classroom and their role in it that will enable them to work effectively.

But the legacy of knowledge-transmission is pervasive; it is embedded in the institutions that prepare teachers and the schools in which they will work. When contributors propose activities that emphasize learners-of-teaching making sense of what they think and do in teaching and learning, these contributors are sowing seeds of change. This book represents a departure from the knowledge-transmission model of teacher education, in which learners-of-teaching are told what to do in their classrooms.

The activities proposed here teach teaching within a constructivist perspective. They reflect the kind of pedagogy that we want to encourage in second language classrooms. They emphasize exploration and experimentation, risk taking and cooperation, balancing input and reflection, using what learners-of-teaching bring and know, and increasing their autonomy. Both the book itself and the activities it contains encourage the notion that teachers do what makes sense to them and that an important aim of teacher education is to explore, expand, and critique this process of making meaning out of individual practice.

The Format of the Book

The book includes 46 activities. The format is somewhat like a cookbook that introduces each recipe with a picture of the final dish, and then explains how to make it. It was inspired in part by Raymond Clark's *Language Teaching Techniques* (1980; Brattleboro, VT: Pro Lingua), in which each technique is introduced through a six-panel cartoon strip. In using that book, I was struck by how easily and quickly teachers got a sense of the whole of the technique, which then helped them implement it. The idea of advice from the experienced user can be found in Janet Gaston's *Cultural Awareness Teaching Techniques* (1984; Brattleboro, VT: Pro Lingua).

Each activity is laid out in a four-part sequence that takes the reader from a complete, integrated image of the activity in practice, in a particular context with a group of learners-of-teaching, through a skeletal procedure and the reasoning behind it, to advice and suggestions on how to use and/or modify the activity:

- Each activity is introduced by a brief *narrative,* often written in the first person, in which the contributor gives a snapshot of the activity in practice.
- This is followed by a step-by-step *procedure* that lays out how to do the activity.
- Then there is a brief *rationale* that explains why the contributor finds it useful.
- Finally, the contributor speaks as an experienced user of the activity to offer a list of *caveats and options:* words-to-the-wise and suggestions for ways to modify or extend the activity.

- If *references or further reading* are mentioned, these are listed at the end of each activity. We have tried to supply further information of a practical nature while not overburdening the book with references.
- Any activity that uses a *handout* includes a version at the end of the activity that can be easily photocopied.

The Users' Guide to Activities classifies the activities in several different ways to show how they can be used.

A Note on Terminology

The terminology in these contributions represented a real rat's nest, due perhaps to the evolving nature of second language teacher education. In order to achieve some coherence and to make the book more accessible, we have standardized terms in the following way:

- We use the term *activity* to capture the scale of the contribution. Activities are bigger than techniques, such as eliciting information rather than calling on students, but they are smaller than full procedures or program designs.
- We refer to language learners in classrooms as *students*.
- For learners-of-teaching, we use either *trainee* to refer to the preservice teacher who has minimal formal classroom teaching experience, or *teacher* to refer to the practicing classroom teacher. Occasionally, groups are collectively referred to as *trainees* when the activity emphasizes initial professional training.
- Finally, we use *teacher educator* throughout the book to refer to teacher trainers, developers, supervisors, course tutors, and professors. The aim is to emphasize the educative dimension of their role.

Donald Freeman
School for International Training
Brattleboro, Vermont, United States

Users' Guide to Activities

Contributor
Mary S. Scholl
School for
International Training,
United States

Outline

I. Time
   A. Activities designed for use within a single class period
   B. Activities designed for use over an extended period
II. Point in Teaching Career
   A. Preservice
   B. In-service
III. Location
   A. In academic programs
      1. Formats for academic courses
      2. Activities for use in academic course work
   B. In the workplace/language classroom
   C. In settings combining academic input and classroom experience
IV. Means of Learning to Teach
   A. General formats for learning teaching
   B. Interpersonal dynamics
   C. Structuring discussions
   D. Using collaborative work
   E. Activities directed by the teacher-learner
   F. Using audiovisual equipment
   G. Drawing upon a shared experience
   H. Addressing cultural issues
   I. Accessing complex ideas
   J. Planning
   K. Using special skills to learn how to teach: listening, writing, and speaking
V. Underlying Purposes
   A. Training for specific teaching skills
   B. Developing awareness
      1. Observation of teaching
      2. Reflection on learning and teaching
   C. Encouraging teacher as researcher in the language classroom

Time

Activities designed for use within a single class period

Activities designed for use over an extended period

Point in Teaching Career

(Activities which apply to *both* preservice and in-service are not included in the lists below.)

Preservice

In-service

Location

In academic programs

Formats for academic courses

Activities for use in academic course work

In the workplace/language classroom

In settings combining academic input and classroom experience

Means of Learning to Teach

General formats for learning teaching

Interpersonal dynamics

Structuring discussions

Using collaborative work

Activities directed by the teacher-learner

Using audiovisual equipment

Drawing upon a shared experience

Addressing cultural issues

Accessing complex ideas

Using special skills to learn how to teach

• listening

• writing

• speaking

Underlying Purposes

Training for specific teaching skills

Developing awareness

Observation of teaching

Reflection on learning and teaching

Encouraging teacher as researcher in the language classroom

Users' Guide to Handouts

Looking at How Discussions Work

Contributor
Marti Anderson
*School for
International Training,
United States*

Narrative

In my teaching of teachers I value the learning that takes place in discussions. I realize that I have certain expectations of what attitudes and activities need to be present in order for a discussion to be fruitful. Recently, I have begun working with my trainees in my teaching methodology class in a way that makes my expectations more explicit and allows trainees to examine these expectations and their own experiences in the discussions that take place in our class.

When trainees arrive on the first day of my methods class, they see on flip chart paper a bubble diagram of my view of the important attitudes and activities that need to be present for our class discussions. To create this diagram, I begin by putting the terms *learning* and *discussions* in the center of the paper. I branch out to the various elements that are represented in my view of discussions such as *listening, understanding, suspending judgment, questioning, silence,* etc. (A sample bubble diagram appears below.) I present my diagram to the class as a part of the overview to the course.

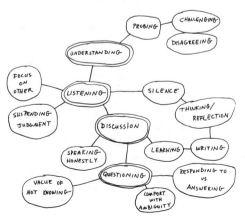

1

Trainees have the opportunity to question my choices and my use of words. Julie asks, "What do you mean by '*suspending judgment*'? Do you mean that we shouldn't have any opinions?" I respond and clarify by saying, "No, I mean that I think it is critical to wait to judge an idea as good or bad until you have had time to sit with the idea and hear what others have to say about it."

Once trainees indicate that they feel they have understood what needs to happen in discussions, I ask that they write reflectively on what they will need to do in order to participate in discussions in this manner. Through reflecting and writing, Julie realizes that suspending judgment is not something she normally does in a discussion and therefore that this will be a challenge to her. Another trainee, Richard, discovers that listening to others is less important to him than voicing his own ideas. He realizes that being a better listener will require attention on his part, that he will have to consciously choose to listen rather than to speak.

After this reflection phase, all the trainees mill around my diagram. They write their names and comments on or near any of the bubbles which they have identified as loci of their work. As this happens, both the trainees and I can begin to see where they have similar concerns and questions, and where we will need to work together to improve discussions. Julie discovers that there are two other people who feel they'll also have trouble in suspending judgment. Richard finds another trainee who will have to work on remembering to listen to others. The diagram is left up in the classroom for the duration of the course and trainees can look at it as they come and go to and from the classroom.

After a couple of class discussions, we revisit the diagram to see what new insights and ideas have emerged. This time, trainees receive their own copy of the diagram. For homework, they add, delete, or create an entirely new diagram representing (a) what they have been experiencing in our class discussions and (b) what *they* think is crucial to fruitful discussions. Trainees bring to class brightly colored diagrams, which they share in small groups. They work in the groups first to understand each other's diagrams and then to compare and contrast their diagrams with mine and their peers'. Julie's diagram has *suspending judgment* in a much smaller bubble than mine. She has highlighted *expressing opinions* and *being listened to* as being of paramount importance. Richard, working in the same group, has added *comfort with conflict* and *liking other group members* to his diagram.

In the large group, we talk about striking similarities and differences. We begin to get to the heart of what makes our discussions work, and the group is struck by the challenges and opportunities of working with differing styles and beliefs, as represented by the personal diagrams.

Once the course is past the midway point, we come back to the diagrams. This time, the trainees make changes to their own diagrams, highlighting elements that have emerged as particularly important and eliminating elements that have lost prominence. We discuss why trainees made the changes they did. Richard has *listening* highlighted in big red letters. He says that he is discovering how much he needs to have his ideas listened to and that this is demonstrating to him the importance of listening in discussions. He notes, "Not everyone can be spouting ideas all the time. Someone has to listen."

As the course draws to a close, we take a final look at the diagram. Trainees write reflectively about their experience with the class discussions and relate this experience to discussions in general. Richard's attitude has shifted dramatically. He now says, "I need to make sure that people are listening to each other. I need to find a way not only to encourage my trainees' expression of their ideas but also to help them see that listening is equally important." These teachers are now more conscious of their beliefs about discussions.

Procedure

1. Prepare a diagram on flip chart paper to demonstrate your beliefs and ideas about discussions.
2. In the first class meeting, present this diagram to the trainees, allowing for time to question and understand the diagram.
3. Ask trainees to write reflectively on their own experiences in participating in discussions and to note for themselves where they think they will need to work relative to the teacher trainer's diagram.
4. Leave up the diagram for the duration of the course.
5. At the end of the first class meeting, have trainees write their names and comments on the large diagram next to the areas where they feel they will need to work.

6. After the group has participated in two or three discussions, ask the trainees to reflect on their experience. They do this by working from their own copy of the diagram as homework. They may add, delete, or create an entirely new diagram that reflects (a) their experience thus far in the class discussions and (b) their beliefs and understanding of how discussions work. Using two colors of ink to represent Steps 1 and 2 is useful.
7. In class, ask trainees to share the diagrams in small groups, working to understand each other's diagram and then to look for similarities and differences.
8. In the large group, discuss similarities and differences.
9. After the midway point of the course, revisit the diagrams. Ask the trainees to refer to their personal diagrams to make any changes or additions.
10. In discussing the diagrams, focus on why trainees made the changes they did.
11. In the final week of the course, ask the trainees to write reflectively on (a) their experience in class discussions in the course and (b) generalizations they can make about the nature of a "good" discussion.
12. Encourage trainees to state what they hope to do about discussions in their own classrooms.

Rationale

Most teacher educators believe that classroom discussions are important and often plan their classes to include them. Training teachers offers a golden opportunity to use the class discussions as a laboratory for understanding more about the nature of discussions themselves and for the trainees to begin to articulate their own sense of what works in discussions. I believe that doing so allows our discussions to be more exciting and fruitful, and gives the trainees some real experience in analyzing and talking about discussions. By making explicit my own expectations and beliefs about the nature of "good" discussions, I allowed my trainees to see what I was doing with them in a more complete way, thus giving them an experience upon which they could build in their own teaching.

Caveats and Options

1. An alternative is to have trainees create their own bubble diagrams before presenting your ideas. In this way, you can gain a clearer perspective on what their thinking is as they enter the course, before it has been colored by what you "the teacher" think. The trainees can share their diagrams with each other and with you. Then you can introduce your ideas and you and the class can see what is complementary or contradictory.

2. In focusing explicitly on discussions, there can be the "can't see the forest for the trees" phenomenon, that is, that the trainees focus so much on *how* they are discussing that they lose sight of *what* they are talking about. I have counterbalanced this phenomenon by holding such "process-oriented" discussions only three times (a total of about 4 1/2 hours) during a 60-hour course. Even so, trainees state that they leave the course with a much greater understanding of the nature of discussions.

3. I have used this process with equal success in courses on other topics and believe that it can work in any teaching context where discussions are used to explore ideas.

Acknowledgments

My colleague Leslie Turpin deserves credit for having come up with the idea of using a bubble diagram to demonstrate her view of discussions and for first using it as a tool in her classes.

Using Student-Selected Readings in a Teacher Education Course

Contributor
Kathleen Bardovi-Harlig
Indiana University,
United States

Narrative

The course, Linguistics Resources and TESOL, is part of the program in Applied Linguistics/TESOL at Indiana University, Bloomington. Students typically take this course in the last semester of the program. This activity gives trainees the responsibility for setting part of the course syllabus.

As a regular part of the course each semester, trainees select articles on designated topics to be included in the syllabus that is read by their classmates. Students also lead small-group discussions about their articles.

In the first week of class, trainees join one or two of six interest groups based on skill areas: pronunciation, listening comprehension, conversation, grammar, reading, and writing. The task of these interest groups is to choose two or three articles for the entire class to read and discuss. The ideal number of participants in each group is four to six. When the class is small, trainees join two groups so that more trainees participate in selecting the readings for each area.

Group members select at least two articles to present to the interest group. The primary criterion for selection is trainee interest. They may select chapters from anthologies or articles from professional journals. Although *TESOL Quarterly* and *TESOL Journal* are obvious sources, I encourage a variety of sources by providing trainees with the list of journals compiled by Diane Larsen-Freeman (1985). After they make their selections, the interest groups convene and members present their selections to the group and discuss why they should be included in the class readings. By the end of the second week or beginning of the third week, the groups have selected two or three articles, with complete bibliographic citations, which they give to the teacher educator, who then compiles the packet and makes arrangements for distribution.

The first small-group discussion of the trainee-selected readings takes place in the fourth or fifth week of class. The day and topic is listed on the course syllabus under the heading "Student-Selected Reading," so the course sequence can be set independently of the particular readings chosen. Each of the discussions are scheduled 1 week apart. The class divides into discussion groups, which are not identical to the interest groups, with one or two members of the designated interest group in each as discussion leaders. All trainees are responsible for the readings, but the interest groups are responsible for leading the discussions. The teacher educator joins the groups as a visitor so as not to divert authority from the trainees.

Procedure

1. Early in the course, list interest sections by topic.
2. Have trainees select an interest section in class. Balance the groups by asking for second choices if necessary. In small classes, have trainees select two interest sections.
3. Direct interest groups to arrange a meeting time.
4. Have each trainee select two articles in the area of interest as homework outside class.
5. When interest groups meet outside class, ask trainees to present their two articles and tell the group why the articles should be read by the entire class. Groups vote on the articles to be selected for the course packet. Each group selects two or three articles.
6. Ask groups to give you a clear reproduction of each article with complete bibliographic information. Prepare the packet and make arrangements for distribution.
7. Assign members of each interest group to lead small-group discussions in class on the materials they selected.

Rationale

Everyone concerned benefits from the activity. The trainees benefit from empowerment. As teachers, they will be responsible for their own continued education in the field, and this activity helps them shift from externally driven education to self-motivated professional development. Selecting the readings for the course allows trainees to take responsibility for their education; it also teaches them where to go as professionals for information on developments in the field. They are encouraged to consider what they want their classmates to know because they determine the readings for the whole class, not just themselves—which distinguishes the project from projects during which trainees work alone. As my colleague Richard Bier observes, when trainees engage in committee work for the purpose of materials selection, they engage in a task that is common in ESL programs. This task demands that group members make individual decisions, defend those decisions, lobby for their positions, and come to a consensus.

Caveats and Options

1. I have chosen to make the readings supplemental to those I choose as the basic readings prior to the start of the class.
2. Another variation is to use a predetermined list of readings from which each of the groups choose two. Although this is not ideal because trainees do not learn about sources for their professional development, it may be necessary when there are limited library holdings at the training site. In such cases, the teacher educators can have trainees choose articles from a personal or departmental collection, if one exists.
3. This activity allows trainees to control part of the content of their methods course, and it allows teacher educators to participate in discussions arranged by the trainees. It is an example of mutual learning from peers.
4. Depending on the format of the course, material from the trainee-selected readings may be included in course assignments, activities, or examinations.
5. In selecting the readings, each trainee reviews several articles and/or journals to make a selection. I have observed that trainees often borrow from each other articles that were not selected by the group to read individually.
6. The teacher educator also benefits from the changing viewpoints. Some semesters trainees select very practical readings; other semesters, they select research or experimentally oriented readings. I take a hands-off approach to the selections. When asked for my advice, I offer guidelines for the selection, but do not participate in choosing the articles. The result is an interesting variety of readings from semester to semester. It is enjoyable to read what trainees have chosen for themselves and it also gives me insight into their interests

and perceived needs. In any single semester, I find that I have read about half of the articles in the course of preparing for classes or reading new issues of journals; the rest I read for the first time with the trainees.

References and Further Reading

Larsen-Freeman, D. (1985, August). Journals of interest to TESOL members. *TESOL Newsletter,* pp. 15-22. (For update, see: Judd, E., & Silberstein, S. [1993, April]. *Getting published: Demystifying the process.* Presented at the 27th Annual TESOL Convention, Atlanta, GA; available from TESOL)

Collaborative Diary Keeping

Contributors
Mark N. Brock, Matilda
M. W. Wong, and
Bartholomew Yu
*City Polytechnic of
Hong Kong, Hong Kong*

Narrative

Diane, Aaron, and Samuel each teach intermediate reading, writing, and listening skills to students in the English Language Center of a large public university. The three teachers have decided to participate in a collaborative diary-keeping project in order to examine their classroom teaching experiences. Each has chosen one course to reflect on through regular diary entries, written immediately after each class meeting.

Today, Samuel has just finished the intermediate writing skills class, which is the topic of his diary entries. He returns to his office and begins writing about his concern with the way he structures group activities in this class. He writes that he is unsure if he should continue grouping the students himself or allow them to form their own groups. After about an hour, he finishes the entry and makes copies for Diane and Aaron.

The next morning, Diane and Aaron respond to Samuel's diary entry. Diane reads Samuel's diary entry and writes, in a short response, that she too is sometimes unsure of the best way to structure group work in her classes. She suggests that they each try grouping students and allowing students to group themselves to see which seems to work best. She also suggests that they discuss this question at their weekly meeting on Friday afternoon. Diane makes two copies of her response, giving one to Samuel and the other to Aaron. On Friday afternoon, Diane, Aaron, and Samuel meet in the teachers' lounge to discuss their entries and the responses they have written during the week. The discussion begins with Samuel expressing frustration that group activities in his writing skills class never seem to work as effectively as he thinks they should. After an hour of discussion about this and several other issues prompted by their entries and responses, the meeting ends.

Procedure

1. Participating teachers arrange a meeting to discuss the kinds of topics they may write about and the kinds of responses they will make to one another's entries. The topics might include classroom management, general teaching approach, rationale for specific teaching approaches, student responses, teacher-student relationships, classroom interaction, teacher decision making, specific "problem" students.
2. Each teacher makes a diary entry immediately after class. They distribute copies to the other teachers in the project. The teachers respond to the entries as soon as possible. Responses to diary entries may include relating one's own experiences; highlighting major issues in the diarist's entries; encouraging, complimenting, and empathizing with the diarist; or offering alternatives.

3. The teachers meet weekly to discuss this project. The weekly discussions among participants may take the following forms: (a) free discussion of any issue arising from the weekly diary entries and responses, (b) discussion of a common or previously agreed-upon issue, (c) discussion of how the diary-keeping experience is affecting participants' teaching.

Rationale

Teachers' work lives are often lived in autonomy and isolation, behind the closed doors of individual classrooms (Lightfoot, 1983). Collaborative diary keeping can play an important role in developing solidarity among teachers by providing a forum to reflect on some of the hidden variables affecting the way they teach. It also offers an opportunity to gain an inside perspective on other teachers' experiences.

The activity has the potential of raising teachers' awareness of classroom processes and prompting them to consider those processes more deeply. The activity also offers a way in which teachers can observe one another's teaching from a "safe distance." It also provides an environment in which teachers can offer one another encouragement and support and share some of the successes and failures they experience in their teaching.

Caveats and Options

1. Teachers who participate in collaborative diary keeping must be able to commit a significant amount of time to the discipline of diary keeping and sharing. They must be willing to relate both pleasant and unpleasant classroom experiences and be committed to working together to gain a clearer picture of classroom teaching and learning processes.
2. Teachers should not view collaborative diary keeping as an evaluative exercise but as an opportunity to learn more about themselves as teachers and the ways in which they teach.
3. It is helpful to write honestly and to be nonjudgmental in response to colleagues' diary entries.

References and Further Reading

Brock, M. N., Yu, B., & Wong, M. M. W. (1992). Journaling together: Collaborative diary-keeping and teacher development. In J. Flowerdew, M. Brock, & S. Hsia (Eds.), *Perspectives in second language teacher education* (pp. 295–307). Hong Kong: City Polytechnic of Hong Kong.

Lightfoot, S. L. (1983). The lives of teachers. In L. Shulman & G. Sykes (Eds.), *Handbook of teaching and policy* (pp. 241–260). New York: Longman.

Taking a Closer Look at the Questions Teachers Ask

Contributor
Elizabeth Byleen
University of Kansas,
United States

During a class hour, teachers ask many questions that, if asked effectively, encourage students to think, stretch, respond, and interact. It is important for teachers to become aware of the power or lack thereof in their questions. With beginning teachers, teacher educators observe classes in a holistic way and give numerous suggestions and tips on classroom management and basic procedures. However, when teachers have refined many basic classroom techniques, it can be useful to delve more deeply into one specific component. Oral questions are an interesting and important aspect to isolate and analyze.

Narrative

After making arrangements with the teacher to observe a class, I go into the ESL classroom and write down all the questions, verbatim, that the teacher asks during the class. I also include the time, perhaps marking every 5 minutes or the beginning of each activity. This involves a lot of fast writing, and I develop my own shorthand as I go along. The number of questions a teacher asks during the hour depends greatly on the type of lesson plan the teacher has, for example, whether she is leading the entire class in a discussion or whether she has planned small-group activities that allow students to interact with each other. In one writing class, a small sample of questions I wrote down looked like this:

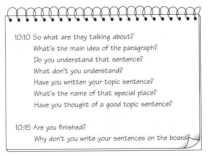

10:10 So what are they talking about?
What's the main idea of the paragraph?
Do you understand that sentence?
What don't you understand?
Have you written your topic sentence?
What's the name of that special place?
Have you thought of a good topic sentence?

10:15 Are you finished?
Why don't you write your sentences on the board?

Notice that the focus is only on the questions; I didn't write the answers down nor did I give the wait-time. However, as a trained observer, I get a good feel for these things by being in the classroom.

After the observation, I give the list of questions to the teacher. Because my handwriting is hurried and not extremely neat, I type them up. I set up a time to discuss the transcript with the teacher in the next few days. Before the meeting, we both spend time analyzing this corpus of data; at the meeting, we both share what we have discovered from the questions and set goals for future exploration.

Procedure

1. Set up a convenient observation time with the teacher.
2. Observe the class and write down all the questions asked.
3. Type the list to make it presentable and give it to the teacher. Explain the task of analyzing the questions. (See Rationale and Caveat 2.)
4. Set up a time to meet with the teacher. To prepare for your meeting, you and the teacher should analyze the data independently.
5. Meet to discuss the teacher's overall reaction to the data. Discuss positive and interesting aspects of the questions as well as areas to improve and how this can be done.

Rationale

This selective verbatim technique (see Acheson & Gall, 1987) gives teachers an opportunity and responsibility to analyze an important part of their teaching; I have discovered that they find this very stimulating. Teachers analyze to varying depths, but all the teachers I have worked with have found positive areas and areas to refine.

The transcripts are rich in areas important to successful teaching. Some of the areas I have discussed with teachers are

1. The ratio of teacher-talk and questioning to student-talk and questioning
2. The logical progression of questions to a desired outcome
3. The intellectual intensity of the questions, in other words, how much they demanded of the students' cognitive processes
4. The balance of question types
5. The clarity of question

6. The appropriateness of vocabulary and grammatical complexity for the language level of the students in the class
7. Who the questions are addressed to, for example, to individual students, the entire class, or anyone who wants to respond, and how issues like seating, gender, or student personalities or cultural mannerisms may affect the distribution of questions in the class
8. Individual speech mannerisms that the teacher desires to lessen or eliminate, for example, intonation that does not clearly signal a question, excessive repetition, or the ubiquitous OK.

Caveats and Options

1. Undoubtedly many areas will come up in discussions, and I think it is best for the teacher to arrive at the focus independently and not use the above list as a starting point for analysis.
2. You could use this selective verbatim approach to focus on positive reinforcement, how directions are given, the introductions and/or conclusions to activities, or transitions.
3. With this activity, the joy is in the analysis and in seeing how teachers analyze their own questions. I have found that almost everyone has derived something important and practical from the analysis. However, occasionally you will work with someone who has very weak analytical skills and who may want you to simply explain what it all means. I think such individuals profit from being guided and given more opportunity and responsibility to analyze their own teaching.

References and Further Reading

Acheson, K., & Gall, M. (1987). *Techniques in the clinical supervision of teachers: Pre-service and inservice applications* (2nd ed.). New York: Longman.

Carlsen, W. (1991). Questioning in classrooms: A sociolinguistic perspective. *Review of Educational Research, 61*(2), 157–178.

Cazden, C. (1988). *Classroom discourse: The language of teaching and learning.* Portsmouth, NH: Heinemann.

Group Teaching a Class

Contributor
Lynne Cameron
*The University of Leeds,
United Kingdom*

Narrative

A trainee stands in front of a class of 7-year-olds in the north of England, questioning children and summarizing their ideas. She writes on the board the children's evaluations of how they had listened to each other in small groups. Watching the scene from the back of the room are five other trainees, their teacher educator (who is the college tutor), and the cooperating teacher. They have all worked together to plan this lesson and to design the questions to be put to the children, and they have agreed on a new way of recording the outcomes. Later the same morning they will meet together to discuss what happened when their ideas were put into practice, and how they—the team—should build on the morning's lesson in the following week's session.

The lesson is one of a series of eight that the team has planned, delivered, and evaluated. Each team member takes a turn at directing the whole class, just as each member chairs the discussion afterwards and writes minutes of the meeting. The topic for the lessons has evolved in a meeting of cooperating teacher, teacher educator, and trainees in which the cooperating teacher nominated listening skills as an area of language development the children needed to work on. The trainees, all studying English Language and Education, had become enthusiastic about a series of lessons in which the children made a video. They felt that the planning and filming would provide opportunities for meaningful group talk and listening. The teacher educator had gone along with the idea, putting forward a few potential problems from her previous experience, but trying not to undermine the group decision. As the weeks went by, the teacher educator had many functions to perform in the group: reminding trainees of the theory that they had read and were now seeing in action, pointing out that there might be a gender issue in the willingness of boys and girls to use the equipment, producing ideas when old ones had dried up, and keeping up spirits when the sound quality of the voices proved too poor to use.

Throughout this process, the teacher educator had to remember that she too was a member of the team with equal but different responsibilities. The class cooperating teacher, who was quite new to teaching, and the class, learned from the close interaction of the team with individual children, seeing them in new situations and discovering new sides to personalities. He gave the trainees short- and long-term strategies for dealing with children and creating learning opportunities. The trainees worked on the close detail of teaching: What will happen if I ask this question? How can children talk about their listening? Why does this child not listen and how can I help? They had time and expert help to ponder the effect of their input, to discuss children's learning, and to evaluate.

Procedure

1. Three months in advance, make arrangements between the school and the college to decide on the class to be involved in the work.
2. One week before, you, the cooperating teacher, and a group of six trainees meet for 3 hours to get to know each other, the school context, the needs of the children, and the requirements of the curriculum.
3. During the first week, you and the trainees visit the school and spend half the morning observing the class and working with small groups. Spend the second part of the morning in discussion, comparing observations, and deciding on the teaching program for the course and the next week.
4. From then, the format will be the same for this session each week: One member of the team acts as chair, one as secretary. You and the cooperating teacher contribute to the discussion as equal members but with your own individual foci. You both offer expertise in class management, knowledge of individual children, and a link between what happens in real classrooms and in educational and linguistic theory.
5. During Weeks 2–9, the first half of the morning is spent with the class. One member of the team leads the delivery of the session planned the previous week. The others observe agreed-upon student

behaviors or activities. The focus of these observations is on the children's learning and on teamwork. Trainees have the opportunity to watch various people at work, including the teacher educator and cooperating teacher, and learn from this. Follow up with the evaluation and planning meeting, as in Step 4.

6. During Week 10, the whole team meets to evaluate the course, assisted by data, including recordings and transcriptions of children, minutes of the evaluation meetings and initial objectives. The discussion ranges over the whole teaching context, from individual children's behavior and use of language to large educational issues, such as the role of group work in developing language skills.

Rationale

This experience comes after trainees have spent 2 full years in college, learning about education and about their academic subject, and after two blocks of time in school as trainees. It brings together in a manageable context the theory and practice they have acquired and provides focus on how individual children learn and how decisions of teachers can control, guide, or hinder them.

For cooperating teachers, the activity provides an opportunity to step back slightly from everyday pressures and observe children. The team discussions also provide an update on educational theory. For the teacher educator, the technique provides a return to the classroom and teaching as well as a chance to work closely with a small group of trainees in an apprenticeship situation.

Caveats and Options

1. The activity only works if the team works. It requires commitment from everyone and sometimes delicate intervention by the cooperating teacher and teacher educator. Trainees must be allowed space to express their ideas and try them out; at the same time, the children's learning must be the priority.

References and Further Reading

Corney, G., & Pendry, A. (1992, April). *Understanding teacher learning through collaboration: A British case study.* Paper presented at the 1992 American Educational Research Association Annual Meeting, San Francisco, CA.

Trainee-Directed Seminars

Contributor
Joan G. Carson
Georgia State University, United States

Narrative

The topic for the evening's sociolinguistics class is "Varieties of Language: Dialect and Ethnicity," and the trainees have read two articles in preparation. Wally, one of the trainees in the course, has arrived early and is nervously arranging chairs, checking the video, and talking quietly to a few trainees about how he wants the class to run tonight. When everyone settles in, the teacher educator makes a few announcements about upcoming assignments and departmental news, and then turns the class over to Wally, who will be in charge of the session.

Wally begins by passing around a three-page handout describing what he intends to do in the 2 1/2 hour class. He briefly goes over his plan and then asks his participants to take a 5-minute self-test that is on the first page of his handout. The test is a series of true-false and multiple choice questions that have been taken from Part 5, "Black on White," of the U.S. public television series *The Story of English* (Cran, McCrum, & MacNeil, 1986). The questions are intriguing; Wally has designed them to draw his peers into the video.

When they finish the test, the class settles in to watch "Black on White," to try to find the answers to the questions they did not know, and to explore some topics of Black English that Wally has culled from the video and listed on the handout. After watching the video, they take a break, and then Wally calls them back together for group discussions. He has written six discussion questions on the handout, questions that explore issues raised in the video or covered in the readings for the class. Wally identifies six discussion leaders and asks the trainees to form discussion groups according to the question they are most interested in talking about. Groups form and talk, and Wally goes from group to group monitoring the discussions. When he is satisfied that groups are reaching closure, he asks the class to come together to give brief summaries of the topics discussed in each group. The summaries generate additional discussion from the whole class, but Wally keeps the group on task and on time.

After all groups have reported, Wally asks the class to think about and discuss one last question: Considering the studies they have read about and discussed today, what are the implications for language teaching and learning in the TESOL context? Too soon the time is up, and Wally asks the teacher educator to say a few words in conclusion. The class ends with the trainees applauding Wally for having prepared and run such an interesting class.

Procedure

1. Make each trainee responsible for organizing and leading the discussion for one of the course topics. A topic includes all the readings assigned for that class; a topic must integrate the readings around the theme.
2. As discussion leader, the trainee is responsible for working out the class format. These responsibilities include:
   a. Providing a handout of (i) how the trainee intends to structure the class and (ii) the points to be covered in the class discussion
   b. Setting up the presentation of the topic
   c. Determining the structure of the discussion and what participants will be asked to do.
3. Ask the trainees to contact you in advance for two things:
   a. To arrange for any audio-/videotapes and equipment
   b. To request that you lecture, which is an option available. If you are asked to lecture, the trainee must specify what material is to be covered and how the lecture will fit in the context of the whole class.
4. Finally, remind the trainees that their role is not to lecture, summarize, or explain the course readings, but rather to find ways for all the trainees to engage directly with the material. If the discussion leaders plan activities such as a video, or a lecture from the professor, they are asked to consider carefully why either or both of those activities make sense in a seminar setting.

Rationale

This activity's structure evolved from my desire to accommodate different learning styles among trainees in my course and to utilize a seminar format. I particularly wanted to avoid a lecture format because I felt it was important to model for trainees what I believed to be true of learning and teaching: that different learners have different needs and goals in any one class and that people learn best when they are responsible for their own learning. This activity allows for various types of class structures and approaches to the material which can accommodate different learning preferences. Trainees who hate group work can plan classes that have none. Trainees who need me to lecture can ask that I do so in their classes. Thus, the activity gives each of the trainees an opportunity to work with and experience various teaching techniques that focus on group interaction.

Caveats and Options

1. Trainees need a chance to look at the topics before they choose the class they will teach. In my courses, they receive the syllabus the first day of class, along with a brief description of the topics to be covered. I ask trainees to read over the topic descriptions I have prepared and select a topic at the next class.
2. It helps to model a few classes before trainees are asked to do them. Either I do the modeling or I ask a trainee who has been in a class with me previously to select the first topic and model it.
3. When there aren't the same number of trainees as there are topics, I may ask them to lead more than one class (when there are few trainees enrolled); or to work as teams (when there are large numbers).
4. It is important to be explicit about how much advance notice you expect when being asked to prepare a lecture. At first, my trainees thought that the material was all prepackaged in my head. They were surprised to hear I could not just pull together a lecture 10 minutes before class. If I am asked to do so, the lectures are on trainee-requested topics so I can be sure that the material needs more explanation than the text provides. In effect, trainee requests and specifications screen out material that might be repetitions of text that they have understood clearly.
5. Trainees often expect that their classes will follow a certain plan and/ or timetable and can get anxious about making sure that the class

conforms to their schedule. It helps to talk about the value of being flexible if and when it is appropriate and to remind trainees to exercise caution when interrupting learning with teaching.

6. Make it clear if you want to be included in class activities. Trainees can feel awkward about assigning their professor to a discussion group so it is best to indicate at the beginning of the course if you want to be a class participant. As a participant in class discussions, I am able to screen trainee comments for misperceptions or inaccuracies and to guide or inform class discussion with my own contributions.

7. Not being in charge of the class can leave you in an awkward position when you want to say something specific to the class. In this case, I contact the discussion leader in advance to request that I be worked into the class plan. I've never been refused time and I am careful not to abuse the privilege.

References and Further Reading

Cran, W. (Producer), McCrum, R., & MacNeil, R. (Series writers). (1986). *The story of English.* Chicago: MacNeil-Lehrer Productions. (Available from Home Vision, 5547 North Ravenswood Avenue, Chicago, IL 60640-1199. Tel 312-878-2600 or 1-800-826-3456 [only in North America]; formats include VHS and Beta)

The Petals Around the Rose: A Data-Coding Activity

Contributor
Douglas W. Coleman
*The University of
Toledo, United States*

Narrative

I was introduced to "The Petals Around the Rose" by Richard Duke of the University of Michigan at the 1987 Annual Conference of the International Simulation and Gaming Association in Venice, Italy. I have used it to give trainees an intuitive understanding of how one's point of view can affect what one sees.

The activity, as I have adapted it for my applied linguistics course, is structured as a simulation. It is divided into three parts: the briefing, the body of the simulation, and the debriefing. In the briefing, I explain the relationship of the form in which data is coded and the information it retains after coding. For example, in a study of second language learners involving the effect of age on second language acquisition (SLA), the researcher might record information on the ages of the students in one of several ways. For example, one might record the actual ages of the students, the age range into which each falls, or the ranking of the students from oldest to youngest. The choice among these different formats for data coding and what the researcher will be able to see in the data are inextricably bound together.

I tell trainees that they will act as researchers of a phenomenon called *the petals around the rose.* I then let them see a few trial runs of the phenomenon. In each trial, I deal several cards using only the four aces, counted as ones, and the two through six of each suit. On each trial, I announce the measurement of the number of petals around the rose. Five sample trial runs appear below, with the number of petals indicated in each case.

Sample Trial Runs

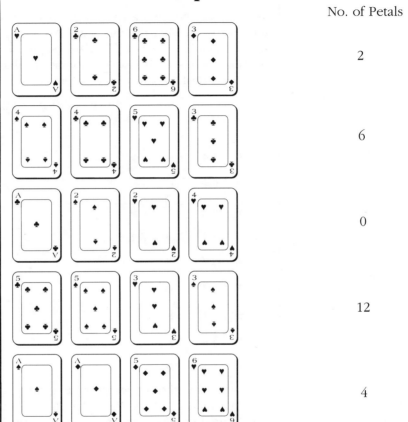

	No. of Petals
	2
	6
	0
	12
	4

Note that by showing you the trials in this way, I have myself used a form of data coding and thereby limited what you can see. If you want to take a stab at figuring out the phenomenon yourself, take a deck of cards and deal the five trial runs so you can see the actual events.

Next, I divide the students into research teams and ask the members of each team to confer and decide on a data-coding format. Then the actual data collection begins. I provide a series of working runs in which I deal the cards onto the overhead and announce the number of petals in each case. As the task proceeds, I gradually reduce the number of cards used on each run and, after a while, announce not only the number of petals but also the number of roses. Using A, 2, 3, 4, 5, and 6 to represent the ranks and club [♣], heart [♥], diamond [♦], and spade [♠], to represent the suits, the display below shows some possible working runs. I urge you to actually deal the cards indicated if you want to figure it out yourself.

Sample Working Runs

				Roses	Petals
4♣	3♠	A♦	2♣	--	2
3♥	5♣	5♠	6♥	--	10
2♥	A♠	A♥	6♠	--	0
6♣	3♦	A♣	2♠	--	2
3♣	5♥	6♥		--	6
A♥	2♣	4♠		--	0
5♣	5♠	2♠		--	8
4♣	3♠	A♦		2	2
3♥	A♣	3♦		3	4

Finally comes the debriefing. Some of the students will have figured out the phenomenon; others will not have. In the debriefing, the students who have figured out the phenomenon explain their "rules." All the students are then invited to discuss their data-coding formats and how these might have hindered their formulation of an accurate rule. We then identify real-life phenomena that could be altered by the way the researcher codes data about them.

Procedure

1. In the briefing, explain the relationship of data coding "information" and the effect of coding on developing hypotheses and conclusions. Introduce the phenomenon, the petals around the rose, as a series of runs and measurements.

2. Give task directions to each group to decide on a data-coding format and then to form a rule to explain the petals around the rose. Perform several trial runs.

3. Do a series of working runs. Display the data by dealing cards or rolling dice, and elicit the student investigators' predictions of the number of petals and, optionally, the number of roses. Then announce the "measurement" of the number of petals and roses.

4. Repeat Step 3 numerous times; after several runs, the number of cards or dice displayed may be reduced to simplify the task; similarly, the number of roses may also be announced to the same end.

5. To debrief the activity, ask student investigators who have solved the puzzle to explain their rules.

6. Ask students to explain their data-coding systems and analyze how these might have hindered their formulation of an accurate rule about the phenomenon.

7. Finally, ask students to identify real-life phenomena that could be distorted by the data-coding formats with which the investigators view them.

Rationale

Once students have been introduced to such concepts of validity and reliability in research, a common next step is to introduce them to aspects of data collection and, in particular, the recording of observations. Although it is possible—even common—for students to develop an intellectual understanding of data collection and how the system they choose for data coding will affect their ability to see different aspects of the phenomenon under study, there may be no useful transfer to their future research practice unless there is also an intuitive understanding as well. This activity provides a kind of experiential encounter designed to foster such transfer.

Caveats and Options

1. Instead of overhead projector "cards," with a small group, I have used real cards or dice. Dice of more than one color may be used, or cards may be dealt so that they lie in a variety of different arrangements; either provides an additional interesting distractor.

2. I usually give a visual clue in the briefing. While explaining the phenomenon to be investigated, I hold out my left hand with fingers touching the thumb, palm up, to represent the rose. I point out the

petals around the edge with the index finger of my right hand. I do this each time I say the phrase.

3. Make sure the students understand that the point of this exercise is not to figure out the petals around the rose but to see how they can make it harder for themselves to figure it out by their own choice of data-coding format.

4. I prepare overhead transparency cutouts of those 24 cards and "deal" them onto an overhead projector.

References and Further Reading

Boglan, R., & Biklen, S. (1982). *Qualitative research for education: An introduction to theory and methods.* Boston: Allyn & Bacon.

Miles, M., & Huberman, A. (1984). *Qualitative data analysis.* Beverly Hills, CA: Sage Publications.

Solution

The cards with a suit symbol—heart [♥], spade [♠], club [♣], or diamond [♦]—in the center, that is the ace, three, and five, are *roses. Petals* are the suit symbols around it: none on an ace, two on a three, and four on a five. On each die face, count the corresponding dots. The phenomenon is spatial, not quantitative.

Using Case Studies in Teacher Education

Contributor
Bill Conley
*School for
International Training,
United States*

Narrative

In a course entitled "Teaching the Four Skills," I use case study descriptions of several different fictional teachers' approaches to teaching listening comprehension. The ability to articulate one's personal approach to teaching each of the four skills is a central goal of the course. The course is organized in a modular format in which each skill is given four classes or roughly 9 contact hours. Each module on each skill begins with an activity in which students have the opportunity to experience the skill in a second language and to reflect on and analyze the processes and subskills they employ in either understanding or producing spoken or written discourse. The single-paragraph descriptions highlight for the trainees different ways that practicing teachers implement their beliefs about the learning and teaching of listening skills and give them a clearer idea of how their own emerging approach to teaching listening compares with those described in the case studies.

After examining the ways in which one processes input by listening in a second language, the trainees do related readings, and on the second or third day of the listening module they are presented with the case studies. In class, the trainees are divided into pairs, given one of the case studies, and told to read it and discuss the fictional teacher's underlying assumptions. After 10–15 minutes of discussion in pairs, the trainees are given a handout with all seven case studies. The pairs then begin reporting their analysis to the large group, and when each pair finishes reporting, the discussion is opened to the large group for comments or alternative interpretations.

As a final step, trainees choose one case study teacher with whom they most identify. Then, going around the room, they take 1 minute to name the teacher whose principles most closely match their own and to explain why. Later the trainees are expected to articulate their assumptions in more detail in a short paper.

Procedure

1. Divide the class into pairs.
2. Give each pair one case study to examine and discuss for 10–15 minutes (see Handout 1).
3. When the paired discussions are finished, distribute a handout with all the case studies on it.
4. Have each pair report their analysis of the particular case study they discussed.
5. After a pair reports, ask for comments and alternative views from the rest of the class on that case.
6. After all the case studies have been discussed, ask members of the class to take 1 minute to name the case study teacher with whom they most identify and explain why.
7. Have trainees follow up this activity by articulating their assumptions about listening in greater detail in a paper.

Rationale

Critical reflection on and analysis of teaching practice is essential in developing teachers who are self-aware and can articulate how theory influences practice and vice versa. One of the best ways for trainees to solidify their thinking and clarify their assumptions is to observe practicing teachers and have time to reflect upon and discuss what they observed. Unfortunately, teacher educators may lack the resources and time to have their trainees observe practicing teachers who are implementing the theories the trainees are currently studying. The case study approach as described above is a way to simulate this process and to allow the teacher educator to assess how trainees are applying theoretical knowledge. I've found that the case studies I've written spark considerable discussion and debate, thus creating an atmosphere in which every member of the class, regardless of teaching experience, can participate on some level. My role in the discussion becomes then truly that of facilitator refereeing and answering questions, if necessary, to clarify case study teachers' actual intentions.

Caveats and Options

1. When composing the case studies, it is important to draw upon your own experience as a teacher or teacher educator. I tried to create authentic cases being careful not to depict examples of either totally abominable or flawless teaching. I tried to integrate into each case some examples of the theoretical constructs we had encountered in our reading about listening.

2. Because the trainees in my course may teach in a variety of settings in the United States and elsewhere, I also included cases of teachers working with students of different ages, grades, and proficiency levels studying different languages.

3. The cases should be detailed enough to give trainees a comprehensive sense of a teacher's overall practice but short enough to read and analyze quickly. One paragraph is the ideal length for each case.

4. Teacher educators can provide more guidance for discussion by including relevant questions for analysis. For example, I wrote the following questions to accompany the case studies so that trainees would consciously analyze the cases according to the theories we had examined:

   a. Does the teacher use interactional- to transactional-type listening materials or a combination of both?

   b. Does the teacher use listening materials that allow students to use bottom-up or top-down processing or a combination of both?

   c. Are the student tasks appropriate designs for responding to the listening text?

   d. Does the teacher use authentic listening materials?

5. Another option I used was to have the trainees meet in groups outside of class to focus on one case study and answer guide. In the next class meeting, each group reported back to the class, which then commented on the analyses.

References and Further Reading

Merseth, K. (1991). *The case for cases in teacher education.* Washington, DC: American Association of Higher Education.

Silverman, R., Welty, W., & Lyons, S. (1992). *Instructor's manual: Case studies for teacher problem solving.* New York: McGraw-Hill.

Handout 1

Case Studies: Assumptions Behind Activities for Teaching Listening

Read the following descriptions of the activities planned by teachers to teach listening. Discuss the assumptions you feel the teacher has about the nature of teaching and learning listening skills.

1. Students in Jan's French II class like just about everything they do in her class except for the dictations given every Friday. Jan selects a passage at random from their text and sometimes from a French newspaper. The dictation usually takes almost the whole 40-minute class period. She doesn't grade them until about a week or two later and the smart kids always get the A's anyway.

2. Ralph had his first-year Spanish students spend 5–10 minutes listening to recorded Spanish in various forms such as poems, news, and weather broadcasts, songs, short conversations, and soap opera dialogues. He didn't require that they do anything other than just relax and "take it in." He will continue to do this throughout the course. On the first day of the course, students listened to tapes of various languages and were asked to detect Spanish and discuss how they were able to identify it.

3. Sara includes a listening activity into every lesson she plans whether the emphasis is on vocabulary, grammar, culture, or pronunciation. She never does listening for its own sake; that is, she never has an entire period of listening activities. Rather she has her low intermediate ESL students work each day on specific graded listening skills such as distinguishing minimal pairs, identifying grammar errors, and

Conley, B. (1993). Using case studies in teacher education. In D. Freeman, with S. Cornwell (Eds.), *New ways in teacher education.* Alexandria, VA: TESOL.

answering specific comprehension questions on culture-specific topics.

4. Bob's busy schedule in the intensive EFL program dictates that he spend 1 of the 5 hours per day on listening. He chooses to have his advanced students watch taped copies of the Bill Cosby sitcom show every day because it's a lot more interesting than exercises in the language lab. After they watch it, Bob asks questions and writes vocabulary and idioms on the board which the students take down and clarify by asking Bob the meanings. Bob tries to work in the vocabulary and idioms into the conversation hour during the week but it's hard to do with all the material they generate after each Cosby episode.

5. Annie's Spanish students at all levels never listen to anything without some preparation for what they will hear, and most of the time she has them perform some simple task to show comprehension. She uses recorded material sparingly, preferring for students to hear live speech spoken by her or the native-speaking guests she brings in least once every 2 weeks. She would like to use video for listening activities, but her school doesn't own a video recorder. Her most common technique with beginners is to start listening activities with questioning and discussion of a picture related to the topic. With more advanced students, she likes to map out the students' ideas on the blackboard on a topic related to the listening activity before they listen. After the listening, she returns to the map and asks them to compare their own thoughts with the information and ideas from the listening passage. Students then listen several more times again to answer both open-ended and specific questions.

6. Joanne teaches ESL in an inner-city bilingual school. She exposes the students to many hours of listening per week by reading aloud stories that the children pick from books in their native language and in English. Read-aloud-time is always followed by the students reading books of their choice in the language that was just read aloud. She has charts on the wall with tips for good listening strategies that the kids designed and painted. She also gives out several Best Listener

Conley, B. (1993). Using case studies in teacher education. In D. Freeman, with S. Cornwell (Eds.), *New ways in teacher education*. Alexandria, VA: TESOL.

of the Day Awards to students and always tells the class what the award recipients did specifically to win the awards.

7. Madeline tries to make sure that the questions she asks at the end of the listening exercise match the type of text she has students listen to. If she has students listen to a short recorded conversation between friends for example, she designs getting-the-gist-type comprehension questions such as determining the topic, setting, the relationship of speakers, main idea, and so on. She does design "search-for-detail-type" postlistening tasks, however. For short texts such as listening to radio ads, she has students ferret out the location, products, and prices of items from a particular type of store. This type of listening is usually followed by a simulated real-life shopping task in class.

Conley, B. (1993). Using case studies in teacher education. In D. Freeman, with S. Cornwell (Eds.), *New ways in teacher education*. Alexandria, VA: TESOL.

Using a Database to Present Whole Language Methodology

Contributor
Lynne Díaz-Rico
*California State
University, San
Bernardino, United
States*

The teachers who participate in an ESL methods course designed for elementary teachers work in school districts in which a whole language teaching philosophy is the accepted paradigm. Some teachers are more knowledgeable and use a wide range of whole language techniques, whereas others are just starting out and have received little guidance in the philosophy. I have found a database a useful tool for equalizing this disparity of experience. It allows teachers to share insights with those currently in the course and with teachers who have taken it previously.

Narrative

I ask teachers to read and evaluate a set of 88 techniques summarized in a packet entitled *Chapter One Reading Instructional Strategies Guide,* prepared by the Albuquerque Public Schools as a summary of whole language instructional methods. Using a standard comment sheet, they enter their opinion of each technique; whether they have used it; if so, if they have found it helpful; if not, if they would recommend any modification of the technique to fit the particular student group they have worked with.

These comments, along with the teacher's name, school, and grade level, are entered into a database using the Macintosh version of Microsoft Works software. A field is created for each of the 88 techniques presented in the packet. Each commentator's opinion of that technique is entered and the techniques are listed in alphabetical order as they are presented in the packet (see samples below).

Sample of Part of the Reading on Assisted Reading

Assisted Reading

Why: Beginning readers and less proficient readers need to be immersed in reading. . . . Paired with a more able reader, the less proficient reader can experience the reading in a positive, nonthreatening way.

Who: Benefits beginning readers and less proficient readers who are reluctant to take risks.

How: . . . Ask the child to read aloud with you. . . . Invite children to join in with a word or phrase whenever they feel they can. . . . Invite children to ask questions about words or parts of words. . . . Do read books over and over again at the child's request. . . .

Sample of Database

Grade Level	Assisted Reading	Name
7, 8	Help limited-English-proficient student gain confidence	Barbra
9-12	Use with peer tutors for ESOL 1, 2	Kirk
Kindergarten	Copies of big books that are read together with partner	Hope
1	Effective to a point when part of a reading conference	Andrea
1, 2	Upper grade peers as reward for good behavior	Mary
Bilingual 1	Dyads or groups of 3-4 could boost self-esteem	Bart

To use the database, a teacher in the class boots up the database disk and elects commentator entries within a narrow grade-level parameter, such as "Kindergarten-1" or "2". The program then selects only those entries that fall within that grade range. Each teacher thus has a wealth of peer advice available, along with hints about suggested implementation or possible modification of the technique to fit the designated grade level. Teachers can preview the techniques they do not currently employ by reviewing others' comments about them.

Procedure

1. Review with teachers the key principles of whole language teaching, particularly as applied to working with ESOL students.
2. Present the packet, containing 88 whole language techniques, with key features noted.
3. Give the teachers an evaluation form and offer sample comments as guidelines for their subsequent commentaries on the techniques.
4. Have the teachers complete an evaluation of the techniques they have used.
5. Enter the comments in the database, making a set of entries for each teacher. The teacher's last name and school are also entered, along with the grade level to which the evaluative comments refer.
6. Ask the teachers to select 10 techniques from the packet upon which to focus. These should be techniques they have found particularly

interesting, either because they currently use them or they are considering the possibility of adding them to their current repertoire.

7. Using the database on a diskette, have teachers work on a self-tutorial basis to check the commentary base on their 10 techniques.
    a. Boot the database. The disk is in read-only mode (i.e., locked).
    b. Teachers enter the file and select those entries matching the grade level they teach; only those selected entries are displayed.
    c. Teachers move the cursor to the vertical column that contains one of the techniques that interests them. Each field containing a comment is expanded to full text size in the text reading window.

Rationale

As with any complex teaching method, practicing teachers do not implement whole language techniques with equal understanding or skill. Many teachers openly solicit the help and wisdom from peers to update their expertise. However, teachers have limited time outside the classroom to converse with each other. Access to a self-tutorial database can be extremely helpful in comparing one's own teaching instincts and experiences with the comments of peers. It is also an excellent means of previewing the use of new techniques and techniques with a particular grade level.

Caveats and Options

1. Teachers with little computer experience will need a step-by-step approach to using the database, more detailed than presented here. A laminated card they can take to the self-tutorial lab listing each step in detail is useful and much appreciated. A demonstration of the database in class is also helpful as is having someone on call who has the database.
2. To create a master list of techniques similar to the Albuquerque list, you could use technique books such as Raymond Clark's *Language Teaching Techniques* (1980; Brattleboro, VT: Pro Lingua); F. Klippel's *Keep on Talking* (1987; Cambridge: Cambridge University Press); Richard R. Day's *New Ways in Teaching Reading* (1993; Alexandria, VA: TESOL); or any other collection of techniques.
3. The database is also a boon to teachers returning to work after a prolonged absence from teaching. Whole language is a relatively recent innovation, and many teachers who have not worked in the field for a while may feel out of touch with it. The database has been

a popular tool for the returning teacher, who may select several promising techniques from the packet and then preview their use with classes ranging from kindergarten to sixth grade.

4. Teachers may bring their own comments with them and add excerpts of their peers' comments if desired.

5. Teachers familiar with the operation of the database program may create a report featuring any of the techniques and print out the comments.

References and Further Reading

Baskwill, J., & Whitman, P. (1986). *Whole language sourcebook.* Toronto: Scholastic.

Cullinan, B. E. (Ed.). (1987). *Children's literature in the reading program.* Newark, DE: International Reading Association.

Goodman, K. (1986). *What's whole in whole language?* Portsmouth, NH: Heinemann.

Goodman, Y., & Burke, C. (1980). *Reading strategies: Focus on comprehension.* New York: Holt, Rinehart & Winston.

Heald-Taylor, G. (1989a). *The administrator's guide to whole language.* Katonah, NY: Richard C. Owen.

Heald-Taylor, G. (1989b). *Whole language strategies for ESL students.* San Diego, CA: Dormac.

Attending to Colleagues: A Technique to Encourage Respect and Development

Contributor
Julian Edge
Aston University,
United Kingdom

Narrative

The teacher educator, John, explains that the aim of the session will be to help group members work with each other. There will be two brief exercises, followed by a discussion of what has happened and what might be learned from them.

John asks the participants to recall a teacher of whom they have strong memories. He then asks the participants to sit in pairs, spreading out to use the available space. In each pair, one person is to be the "speaker" and the other the "understander." The speaker is asked to tell the understander about the teacher he or she has in mind. The understander's task is to make the speaker feel well listened to, but not to speak. Two minutes are allowed for the task. Participants quickly decide on their roles, and there is a buzz of serious talk. When the time is up and the teacher educator brings the group back together, some participants show good-humored displeasure at being interrupted. He now asks them to reverse roles. The speaker's task remains the same. The understander's task, however, is to do everything possible to signal a complete lack of interest in what the speaker is saying, again without speaking. Two minutes are allowed. There is a great deal of laughter around the room. Before the time limit expires, some pairs have given up on the task.

John asks speakers from the first task how it felt to be listened to so intently. A series of points are elicited. He then asks how the speakers felt in the second task, and more points are elicited. He pulls together the points raised and highlights the influence of listeners on speakers. John asks if there are any further comments or questions relating to the tasks.

40

He then elicits response regarding the relevance of this experience to participants' work together, before adding his own thoughts and drawing conclusions.

Procedure

1. The teacher educator explains the purpose of the activity: that participants practice listening skills and that the activity proceed from task to reflection.
2. Ask participants to think of a teacher of whom they have strong memories.
3. Ask participants to move into pairs.
4. Set the first task with a time limit, introducing the roles of speaker and understander. During Task 1, the speaker talks about his or her memories of the teacher (Step 2) for 2 minutes. The understander does not speak, but does everything possible to make the speaker feel well listened to.
5. When the time is up, set the second task, also allowing 2 minutes talk. During Task 2, roles are reversed. The new speaker has the same task. The understander again does not speak but should do everything possible to signal a complete lack of interest in what the speaker has to say.
6. Elicit from the first and second set of speakers in turn how it felt to be listened to in this way.
7. Invite further comment from the participants.
8. Emphasize the power of listeners over speakers in terms of the speaker's motivation and, consequently, over both the quantity and quality of the speaker's communication.
9. Facilitate a discussion of the relevance of this experience to teacher development.

Rationale

The activity, which is taken from a large-scale framework for teacher cooperation described in Edge (1992a, 1992b), emphasizes that respect leads to careful listening in an attempt to understand and thus encourages colleagues' development. This activity is an example of the process whereby *experience* is illuminated by *reflection*, leading to *understanding*, on the basis of which one can prepare *action* (Kolb, 1984).

Caveats and Options

1. For experienced teachers, an alternative to the task content is to ask trainees to recall a class of which they have strong memories. If there is a local issue on which everyone has an opinion, this also works very well.
2. A useful discussion can follow on what it is that a person actually does in order to make someone feel "well listened to."
3. A useful follow-up task with alternative content asks the understander to choose the best words to describe the emotions or attitudes he or she hears in what the speaker has to say. The speaker can then comment on the accuracy of this choice of words.
4. The activity can be usefully related to classroom observation (Freeman, 1982), and can be used to introduce teachers to the ideas of Rogers (e.g., 1983), which underpin so much work in learner autonomy and teacher development.
5. If you have an odd number of participants, ask one person to observe a pair and comment afterwards. If you take part in a pair yourself, you risk missing out on problems elsewhere. This is a teaching decision that you can usefully discuss with participants.
6. You can elicit the first speakers' reactions before reversing roles (Step 5). I have found that having the contrast of both experiences without a break makes it easier to express the contrast in words afterwards.
7. Don't preempt objections or awkward outcomes in the activity. Demonstrate that you can listen and understand. Show respect, and others will respect what you want to say. Note how our own methods must be congruent with what we say. In teacher education, the method is the message.

References and Further Readings

Edge, J. (1992a). Cooperative development. *ELT Journal, 46*(1), 62–70.

Edge, J. (1992b). *Cooperative development: Professional self-development through cooperation with colleagues.* Harlow, England: Longman.

Freeman, D. (1982). Observing teachers: Three approaches to in-service training and development. *TESOL Quarterly, 16*(1), 21–38.

Kolb, D. (1984). *Experiential learning: Experience as the source of learning and development.* Englewood Cliffs, NJ: Prentice Hall.

Rogers, C. (1983). *Freedom to learn for the eighties.* Columbus, OH: Merrill.

Teacher Assessment

Contributor
Alvino E. Fantini
School for
International Training,
United States

I have found that the premises on which teacher assessment is conducted are not always clear and that the criteria may vary from case to case. To make these criteria more explicit in the observation and assessment process, the YOGA Form was developed—the acronym stands for Your Objectives, Guidelines, and Assessment. It is intended to help by clarifying the trainee's or practicing teacher's *objectives*; by providing *guidelines* for periodic monitoring over time; and by establishing a common form of *assessment* for use by the trainee and the teacher educator. Thus, the form addresses how trainees are progressing in teaching, how they teach, and how their skills compare with a series of competencies.

Narrative

As a faculty member in a teacher education program, I am often responsible for observing and supervising trainees. Prior to their internship, I require them to outline their personal and professional goals and objectives for this experience. During the practice teaching period, I visit the trainees' classes periodically to observe and assess their teaching. During these visits, I use the YOGA form to focus attention on more discrete aspects of the learning and teaching process. We each complete the form after my visit and then we discuss it together. As we talk, I emphasize the perceptions each of us is contributing, rather than on who is right or wrong. We end each conference with a brief synthesis of the trainees' strengths as well as areas for their future development. Our exchange is an important element in a cycle of reflection, analysis, synthesis, and action that helps trainees improve their teaching.

When the teaching internship is finished, we meet one last time. It is interesting to look over the YOGA form from our various discussions, to see how each trainee's teaching has developed through the internship, and to complete one last assessment.

Procedure

1. Provide trainees with the YOGA form (see Handout 2) before or early in the teaching internship period and ask them to complete it as a self-assessment.
2. Observe the trainee's teaching and evaluate it using the form.
3. Compare your separate evaluations and discuss your varying perspectives of the trainee's teaching. Conclude the meeting with a summary of strengths and areas for improvement in the trainee's teaching and prioritize objectives—drawn from the form—for the next time period.
4. Repeat this process as often as feasible and/or desirable during the teaching internship. At each visit, employ different marking systems to track the trainee's work: A checkmark [√] is used the first time, a circle [○] the next, and a square [□] the third and so on, or different colored markings can also be used.
5. After the teaching internship is finished, you and the trainee complete the form for the final time. Meet together to summarize the trainee's strengths and areas for improvement.

Rationale

Many pre- or in-service programs prescribe some routine manner of assessing the trainee's or teacher's classroom performance that can often serve as a sort of teacher report card. In recent years, however, the emphasis has shifted from evaluation to staff development in an effort to promote competent and effective teachers committed to a process of continual learning.

To compile this form, I examined approximately 50 forms used by institutions at various educational levels and found that most forms reflected assumptions about teacher competence and assessed teacher performance in specific areas. They typically organized lists of important teaching factors into subsets and included some sort of evaluation system (e.g., Outstanding, Satisfactory, Needs Improvement). Despite the varying items and emphases, however, the forms shared numerous commonalities. The YOGA form is a composite list of the most commonly recurring factors grouped into six competency areas: interpersonal relations, cultural and intercultural knowledge, language and linguistic knowledge, language acquisition and learning, language teaching, and professionalism. These six competencies were developed collectively by the faculty of the Master of Arts in Teaching Program at the School for International Training.

Caveats and Options

1. The YOGA form need not be used on the first visit if you are seeking a more global impression and want to avoid taking notes in order for the trainee and students to feel comfortable with a visitor.
2. At the end of the observation period, you and the trainee can complete an action plan for the trainee's future work that may include reading, action research, focused practice of new techniques, further study or coursework in specified areas, etc.
3. It is important to keep in mind that, despite the rather formidable list on the YOGA form, teaching excellence cannot be ensured simply by checking off a series of discrete tasks. Clearly a checklist, no matter how comprehensive, is only a guide.

Handout 2

The YOGA Form: A Monitoring Aid for Teacher Assessment

The goal of this form is to help those who use it to become competent, effective teachers committed to a process of continual learning. The form is intended to serve in three ways: (a) to identify *objectives* for your teaching, (b) to serve as *guidelines* for periodic reference and evaluation, and (c) as an *assessment* tool. You will want to evaluate yourself periodically and to compare your perceptions with those of your observer as an aid to the conferencing that follows.

Each category provides spaces to add other factors identified by you and/or your observer, not already accounted for in this form. The last page is designed to encourage synthesis and an action plan for further development.

Key

0 = N/A (Not applicable), N/O (Not observed), or
    See written comment(s)
1 = Room for growth/development
2 = Acceptable
3 = Competent

The following six competencies, and many of the indicators included within them, were developed collectively by the faculty of the Master of Arts in Teaching program at the School for International Training; their use in this format is the author's.

Fantini, A. E. (1993). Teacher assessment. In D. Freeman, with S. Cornwell (Eds.), *New ways in teacher education.* Alexandria, VA: TESOL.

I. Inter-personal Relations

Dynamic, enthusiastic, confident about his/her teaching, the students, the subject matter

0/-1 +/-2 +/-3 +

Creates a positive, secure, comfortable classroom ambiance (e.g., where students can take risks)

0/-1 +/-2 +/-3 +

Effective classroom management (e.g., deals with discipline, personality conflicts, student expectations, etc.)

0/-1 +/-2 +/-3 +

Rapport with students:
- knows students and their names

0/-1 +/-2 +/-3 +

- listens to and understands what students are saying (on affective and cognitive levels)

0/-1 +/-2 +/-3 +

- attentive and responsive to *all* students versus particular types (e.g., most vocal, brightest, etc.)

0/-1 +/-2 +/-3 +

- clarifies boundaries for appropriate behaviors and responds to transgressions

0/-1 +/-2 +/-3 +

Promotes good student relationships (e.g., encourages pair and group work, collaboration, sharing, etc.)

0/-1 +/-2 +/-3 +

Encourages student responsibility for own learning and for contributing to class experience

0/-1 +/-2 +/-3 +

Works well with other teachers, supervisor, administrators

0/-1 +/-2 +/-3 +

_____ 0/-1 +/-2 +/-3 +

_____ 0/-1 +/-2 +/-3 +

Fantini, A. E. (1993). Teacher assessment. In D. Freeman, with S. Cornwell (Eds.), *New ways in teacher education.* Alexandria, VA: TESOL.

II. Cultural/ Intercultural Knowledge

Inclusion of cultural dimension in the lessons:
- aware of and attentive to sociolinguistic variables   0/-1 + /-2 + /-3 +
- uses appropriate target language social interactional activities   0/-1 + /-2 + /-3 +
- addresses target language culture through readings, discussions, topics, etc.   0/-1 + /-2 + /-3 +

Presence of cultural dimension in classroom dynamics:
- sensitive to/respects student cultural differences   0/-1 + /-2 + /-3 +
- uses the cultural diversity of students to advantage   0/-1 + /-2 + /-3 +
- fosters students' interest in and understanding of the target culture   0/-1 + /-2 + /-3 +
- creates opportunities for students to experience the target language culture   0/-1 + /-2 + /-3 +
- fosters students' respect for cultural diversity   0/-1 + /-2 + /-3 +

Inclusion of intercultural dimension
- compares and contrasts target and students' own culture(s)   0/-1 + /-2 + /-3 +
- explores intercultural processes   0/-1 + /-2 + /-3 +
- responds to intercultural conflicts if they arise   0/-1 + /-2 + /-3 +

Aware of/sensitive/responsive to intercultural challenges of the teaching situation:
- in the institution   0/-1 + /-2 + /-3 +
- in the community   0/-1 + /-2 + /-3 +

_____   0/-1 + /-2 + /-3 +

_____   0/-1 + /-2 + /-3 +

Fantini, A. E. (1993). Teacher assessment. In D. Freeman, with S. Cornwell (Eds.), *New ways in teacher education.* Alexandria, VA: TESOL.

III. Language/ Linguistic Knowledge

Mastery of target language (for nonnative speakers): fluency, pronunciation, and accuracy of grammar	0/-1 +/-2 +/-3 +
Knowledge of target language phonology and grammar	0/-1 +/-2 +/-3 +
Uses natural and comprehensible language, varying appropriately for different contexts/needs	0/-1 +/-2 +/-3 +

Able to
- present linguistic rules clearly and appropriately   0/-1 +/-2 +/-3 +

- present appropriate amounts of structured material   0/-1 +/-2 +/-3 +

- draw effectively on students' knowledge of and intuition about the target language   0/-1 +/-2 +/-3 +

- respond effectively to students' questions on linguistic points   0/-1 +/-2 +/-3 +

- research linguistic problems/conduct linguistic analysis   0/-1 +/-2 +/-3 +

- recycle grammar periodically to reinforce students' mastery   0/-1 +/-2 +/-3 +

Uses students' native language(s) effectively and judiciously   0/-1 +/-2 +/-3 +

_____   0/-1 +/-2 +/-3 +

_____   0/-1 +/-2 +/-3 +

Fantini, A. E. (1993). Teacher assessment. In D. Freeman, with S. Cornwell (Eds.), *New ways in teacher education.* Alexandria, VA: TESOL.

IV. Language Acquisition and Learning

Identifies and responds to individual student factors (e.g., social, psychological, personality) affecting learning $\quad$ 0/-1+/-2+/-3+

Devises lessons that reflect what is known about successful language learning strategies $\quad$ 0/-1+/-2+/-3+

Adapts teaching to varied individual and cultural learning styles $\quad$ 0/-1+/-2+/-3+

Helps students understand purpose of lesson or activity and relates to student interests/needs $\quad$ 0/-1+/-2+/-3+

Helps students increase awareness of their own acquisition process and what facilitates/hinders their learning $\quad$ 0/-1+/-2+/-3+

Uses varied, timely and appropriate error detection and diagnosis strategies, including self-monitoring $\quad$ 0/-1+/-2+/-3+

Promotes self-learning skills for independent field learning $\quad$ 0/-1+/-2+/-3+

_____ 0/-1+/-2+/-3+

_____ 0/-1+/-2+/-3+

Fantini, A. E. (1993). Teacher assessment. In D. Freeman, with S. Cornwell (Eds.), *New ways in teacher education*. Alexandria, VA: TESOL.

V. Language Teaching

Course Design

Needs assessment:
- addresses the institution or program's pedagogical requirements (as applicable)   0/-1 +/-2 +/-3 +

- considers students' needs, interests, prior knowledge   0/-1 +/-2 +/-3 +

Clearly identifies course goals and objectives:
- addresses skill areas (eg. listening, speaking, reading and/or writing), as appropriate   0/-1 +/-2 +/-3 +

Develops an appropriate syllabus:
- course design and sequence reflect the goals and objectives   0/-1 +/-2 +/-3 +

- considers both course process and content   0/-1 +/-2 +/-3 +

Designs lesson plans appropriate to course design/objectives   0/-1 +/-2 +/-3 +

_____   0/-1 +/-2 +/-3 +

Classroom Environment

Attentive to appearance/physical condition of room   0/-1 +/-2 +/-3 +

Organizes room in varied ways as appropriate to activities   0/-1 +/-2 +/-3 +

_____   0/-1 +/-2 +/-3 +

Fantini, A. E. (1993). Teacher assessment. In D. Freeman, with S. Cornwell (Eds.), *New ways in teacher education.* Alexandria, VA: TESOL.

Lesson Plans and Implementation

Develops lessons with clear objectives which students understand — 0/-1 +/-2 +/-3 +

Provides appropriate content, level and amount of work (e.g., varied, challenging, engaging, etc.) — 0/-1 +/-2 +/-3 +

Initiates lesson with warm-up and review activities — 0/-1 +/-2 +/-3 +

Implements lessons effectively, utilizing inductive/deductive approaches as appropriate — 0/-1 +/-2 +/-3 +

Works effectively with class size (from tutorial to small/large groups) and levels (homogeneous to multilevel) — 0/-1 +/-2 +/-3 +

Uses appropriate and varied teaching techniques/activities, with clear purposes — 0/-1 +/-2 +/-3 +

Displays good timing, pacing, flow, transitions, progression — 0/-1 +/-2 +/-3 +

Engages all sensory modes, as appropriate, to aid cognitive, affective, and psychomotor development — 0/-1 +/-2 +/-3 +

Addresses skill areas as appropriate (e.g., comprehension, speaking, reading, and writing) — 0/-1 +/-2 +/-3 +

Addresses varied aspects of communicative competence (e.g., linguistic, paralinguistic and nonverbal) — 0/-1 +/-2 +/-3 +

Provides clear instructions with students paraphrasing, as appropriate — 0/-1 +/-2 +/-3 +

Adjusts plan appropriately based on how things are going — 0/-1 +/-2 +/-3 +

Moves around room/uses gestures, as appropriate — 0/-1 +/-2 +/-3 +

Fantini, A. E. (1993). Teacher assessment. In D. Freeman, with S. Cornwell (Eds.), *New ways in teacher education.* Alexandria, VA: TESOL.

Maximizes student involvement/participation   0/-1 +/-2 +/-3 +

Varies groupings as appropriate to activities (e.g., individual/pair/small to large group work)   0/-1 +/-2 +/-3 +

Effectively uses resources (e.g., blackboard, texts, audio-visuals, realia, etc.)   0/-1 +/-2 +/-3 +

Uses appropriate correction techniques (e.g., amount, type, timing, students and peers)   0/-1 +/-2 +/-3 +

Designs appropriate homework tasks related to course plan, lesson, amount, quality, timing, etc.   0/-1 +/-2 +/-3 +

_____   0/-1 +/-2 +/-3 +

_____   0/-1 +/-2 +/-3 +

Assessment and Feedback

Conducts appropriate evaluations   0/-1 +/-2 +/-3 +

Assessment is congruent with course objectives, content and process   0/-1 +/-2 +/-3 +

Ensures students understand the evaluation process   0/-1 +/-2 +/-3 +

Uses effective approaches to student assessment   0/-1 +/-2 +/-3 +

Fosters student self- and peer evaluation   0/-1 +/-2 +/-3 +

Develops reliable/valid measures, properly weighted and expressed in terms students understand   0/-1 +/-2 +/-3 +

Uses effective ways of providing feedback to students   0/-1 +/-2 +/-3 +

Establishes appropriate mechanisms to elicit student feedback on teacher's performance and course   0/-1 +/-2 +/-3 +

Fantini, A. E. (1993). Teacher assessment. In D. Freeman, with S. Cornwell (Eds.), *New ways in teacher education.* Alexandria, VA: TESOL.

Evaluation measures students' attainment of course objectives	0/-1 + /-2 + /-3 +
_____	0/-1 + /-2 + /-3 +
_____	0/-1 + /-2 + /-3 +

VI. Professionalism

Expresses self clearly in oral and written communication	0/-1 + /-2 + /-3 +
Complies with policies, procedures, requirements, etc. of school setting	0/-1 + /-2 + /-3 +
Exhibits professional conduct (e.g., punctuality, reliability, appearance, behavior, etc.)	0/-1 + /-2 + /-3 +
Able/willing/interested in assessing own performance	0/-1 + /-2 + /-3 +
Can identify internal/external factors which help/hinder own development as a teacher	0/-1 + /-2 + /-3 +
Seeks/accepts feedback from colleagues, supervisor/observer	0/-1 + /-2 + /-3 +
Develops and pursues action plan for future professional development	0/-1 + /-2 + /-3 +
Maintains appropriate relations with students, colleagues, department, institution, supervisor, host culture	0/-1 + /-2 + /-3 +
Aware of and responsive to the style, philosophy, needs of the institution, the community, the culture in which working	0/-1 + /-2 + /-3 +
Open/shares with others, contributes to the field	0/-1 + /-2 + /-3 +

Fantini, A. E. (1993). Teacher assessment. In D. Freeman, with S. Cornwell (Eds.), *New ways in teacher education.* Alexandria, VA: TESOL.

Promotes general welfare of the teaching profession   0/-1 +/-2 +/-3 +

_____   0/-1 +/-2 +/-3 +

_____   0/-1 +/-2 +/-3 +

Synthesis and Recommend-ations

Strong points:

Areas for further exploration/development:

Fantini, A. E. (1993). Teacher assessment. In D. Freeman, with S. Cornwell (Eds.), *New ways in teacher education.* Alexandria, VA: TESOL.

The Materials/Media Fair

Contributor
Jerry G. Gebhard
Indiana University of Pennsylvania, United States

Narrative

The guests, who include ESL teachers from the language institute, classmates, professors, the college dean, and close friends, enter the very large room. The first thing they see is a banner-sized computer printout with "Welcome to the ESL Materials/Media Fair!" Just inside the door is a table with programs, a sign-in book for guests, and evaluation forms. As the guests wander around the room, they see 20 or so displays. At each, a trainee, who created the project, is explaining, showing, or getting guests involved in a project.

At one table, Hiromi's several guests are sitting at a computer playing a vocabulary game that she has created and programmed. Franklin is at the next table explaining to a small group how to make slides from transparencies. Near him, Ivannia is showing a videotape of children singing ESL songs she wrote. Across the room, Dennis is having guests play IUP (Idiomatic Usage Pursuit), a game based on Trivial Pursuit, except that the categories include such topics as Language Functions, Expressions Used by Teenagers, and Survival English.

Across the room, Liyan is having guests add their own voices to a Charlie Chaplin film, while Ahmad is encouraging guests to study a large read-and-write board on which they study cartoons and fill in the bubbles, read notices and write their own, write in original endings to short stories, and more. In the center of the room, Mohammed is watching guests walk around his culture pyramid. On each wall of the pyramid, he has a variety of information about cultural values, behaviors, and customs. Less obvious, but as impressive, are Porntip's three chapters of an EFL reader for university students, Lilly's original illustrated stories and poems for children, and Lian-Aik's listening activities based on authentic language used in the media.

Sooner or later, the guests focus on a popular display, the international food table, where they can select from a wide assortment of main dishes and desserts. The room is filled with laughter and interest. The once nervous trainees are smiling and conversing with guests; they are confident. Their fair has been a success.

Procedure

1. A month or so before the fair, explain its goal: to provide chances for trainees to create an original materials/media project that they will display at a fair attended by invited guests. Emphasize that the fair is a group effort and, as such, trainees are responsible not only for their own projects but for the fair's organization as well.
2. Give examples of fair projects.

3. Have trainees meet in small groups to brainstorm ideas for projects. Each group has the chance to report on project ideas, which can be listed and explained to everyone.
4. Ask each trainee to write down a few ideas for a fair project.
5. Request that each trainee submit one project idea.
6. Have trainees work independently on their own projects.
7. Have trainees join one or more committees to organize the fair. These include:
   a. The Layout Committee, which designs the display layout and secures equipment (e.g., video monitors, extension cords)
   b. The Program Committee, which collects and edits project descriptions and presenter biographies and designs, prints, and copies the program
   c. The Advertisement Committee, which makes up the guest list, sends out invitations, and creates ads to publicize the fair
   d. The Food Committee, which collects money and arranges for the preparation of the food, and
   e. The Evaluation Committee, which designs, processes, and copies the evaluation and feedback forms.

Rationale

The Materials/Media Fair is a hands-on experience. Trainees can synthesize their knowledge and apply it in the creation of teaching materials. The fair offers trainees a chance to collaborate with a variety of people—classmates, the teacher educator, classroom teachers, and library/resources personnel—thus emphasizing that such collaboration is useful. They should feel free to consult with others rather than isolate themselves.

The fair has a built-in source of motivation. Trainees work hard when they know others will see and evaluate their work. With the support and encouragement of the teacher educator, trainees can go beyond their previous experience to accomplish a project in which they can take pride. Finally, the fair can build a sense of community, especially when the teacher educator stresses a noncompetitive atmosphere. Trainees will help each other on their projects, join more than one committee, and work at making the fair a success. This type of collaboration is needed in the workplace, and if it begins in teacher education programs, there is a greater possibility that teachers will establish stronger collaborative ties in the jobs.

Caveats and Options

1. Some trainees, especially those new to teaching and to materials development, may feel somewhat anxious or insecure about having to display a fair project. To address this, you can suggest that class members pair up to create their fair projects. Another way to reduce anxiety is to limit the guest list to only classmates and close friends, thus making the fair a more intimate occasion.

2. You can meet with each trainee to talk about project ideas and give some direction.

3. Librarians in Media Resources are useful sources for reference books and journal articles on second language materials and media; experts in media and communications, experienced ESL/EFL teachers, and language lab teachers can help as resources as well.

4. Posters developed by trainees can be used to report on classroom issues, action research, curriculum units, and other areas.

5. You can request that trainees write a report on what they have learned in doing this research. Trainees can also write a detailed description of their proposed fair project based on this research, including a step-by-step description of the process to create the project.

Self-Tests

Contributor
Kathleen Graves
School for
International Training,
United States

Narrative

In the English grammar portion of a course called "Teaching the English Language," we have just finished studying the article system, which includes countable and uncountable nouns, quantifiers, and measure words. During this segment of two 2-hour classes, a period of 2 weeks, trainees have read about the article system, talked about it, taken notes about it, done a worksheet on it, and been students in minilessons around different aspects of the article system.

At the end of the second class, I give them a three-page handout titled "Review 4: Count/Noncount/Articles." The review comprises two parts: a knowledge and a teaching section. Here, I will only be referring to the knowledge section. This section includes 10 questions such as

1. What test can you apply to a noun to determine whether it is countable or not? Give examples.
2. Give examples of two nouns that can be either count or noncount. Use them in sentences.

The trainees have a week in which to complete this self-test. They do what they have done with previous reviews. First they answer the questions straight through, on their own. After that, they write at the top of the review, for example, *first time through, green pen*. Then they look through the questions again and this time consult their notes, the text, their classmates, or any other resources available to them. They add to or change their answers as they feel necessary. After the second go round, they write at the top of the review, for example, *second time through, blue pen*. They are also free to write questions to me on the review.

They hand the review in to me. I read through each one. If there are any incorrect answers, I return the review to the trainee to find and provide the correct answers. I also write answers to questions they have asked.

When I hand back the reviews, I also give them a handout titled "Review 4: Count/Noncount/Articles: Some Answers." This handout is identical to the review, but has my answers to the questions in the knowledge section and includes examples drawn from their answers.

Procedure

1. After the completion of a testable segment of a course, distribute a self-test that includes questions drawn from work trainees have done during the segment.
2. Tell trainees when the self-tests are due. Explain that they are to do the self-test once through, on their own, without consulting notes, books, or other aids. When finished, they are to indicate at the top of the review the type of writing implement used. After they have done it once through on their own, they are free to go through it a second time, using a different writing implement, and adding to or changing their answers, as they see fit. On this try, they may consult their notes, each other, the textbook, or any other resources. They indicate at the top of the review the type of writing implement used on the second try. They may also write questions to the teacher on the self-test.
3. When the tests are due, collect and read through them. If a trainee has missed any answers, make a note on the test and return it with a note about the numbers missed, which must be redone, and with a due date.
4. Write your own answers to the questions, using correct examples from the trainees' self-tests.
5. When you return the self-tests, give the trainees the answers you have compiled.

Rationale

I do the reviews this way because I believe it resembles what teachers actually do. They rely on and use the information they already know. When they don't know something, they look it up in references, talk to colleagues, consult notes, etc.

Both the teacher educator and the trainees can tell at a glance which answers on the review they know or have retained, and which they need to supplement or find. For the trainees, it is helpful to know how much they do know and to pinpoint what they don't know. For the teacher educator, it indicates what has been clear, what hasn't, where trainees are on track, and where they are lacking.

These tests are meant to be self-assessments. Their purpose is to offer trainees a sense of what they know and to use the resources available to them to find answers to what they don't know. If these were closed-book tests, the emphasis would be on how many right answers trainees have, rather than whether they know how to find the answers. I call these self-tests *reviews*, partly as a euphemism, but also because they do allow trainees to have another look at what we have just covered in class. The choice of questions shows them what I consider to be important.

My answers, given at the end, serve as another self-check. Seeing their examples included validates their expertise and also binds the class together. Trainees' sense of humor and personalities emerge both for me and for them. One trainee coined the term *modaloid* on one of the reviews, for example, to refer to those auxiliaries that exhibit features of both true modals and periphrastic modals. This term became part of the class lexicon.

Caveats and Options

1. Trainees are usually not used to this way of taking tests. They must be reminded to use two writing implements and the rationale for this way of taking the test must be carefully explained.
2. Trainees have indicated that they prefer to be given these tests regularly after a discrete chunk of material has been completed. I used to give longer tests, which they found overwhelming.
3. It is important to make sure that trainees who have missed answers do them correctly, both to give the message that the test is important and for them to fill in the gaps. Trainees have indicated that redoing the answers has given them a sense of self-confidence and made them realize they can't be sloppy.
4. It is time consuming to compile answers that include examples from their reviews. I have the tests on computer as well as my answers. I generally only need to change the examples. However, if I have

learned something new from working with the students, I also modify my answers to include that knowledge or insight.

5. When students do ask questions on the reviews, it allows me to have a private conversation with them. Nonnative English speakers have said they find this particularly helpful.

The Teaching Game

Contributor
Kathleen Graves
*School for
International Training,
United States*

Narrative

It is the end of the first day of a week-long workshop on instructional objectives. Workshop participants are 16 English teachers in a large binational center in southern Brazil. I give them the following homework instructions: "Prepare a 10-minute lesson in which you teach your colleagues something that is *not* language. You will be in groups of four, so you will have three students."

The next day, I divide the participants into groups of four, each assigned to a different room or hall space, and give them the following instructions on a handout.

The Teaching Game

After each 10-minute lesson, please take 15 minutes to do the following. You will need a timekeeper to tell the teacher when the 10 minutes of teaching are over. Please be strict!

Teacher:
1. Tell your group what your objectives were.
2. Talk about whether you feel the objectives were achieved.
3. If so, explain how you know they were achieved. If not, talk about why you think they weren't achieved.
4. Finally, if you were to do the lesson again, is there anything you would do differently. Why?

Students:
5. Tell the teacher whether you feel you were able to achieve the objectives.
6. Tell her/him what helped you achieve them/hindered your achieving them.

As they do the activity, I circulate. In one group, a teacher is demonstrating a massage technique; in another, a teacher is explaining a recipe. In another group, a teacher is demonstrating and explaining the five ballet positions. At the end of the 10 minutes, they discuss the questions. The "ballet teacher" says that her objective was for the students to learn the five ballet positions. I ask the teacher what she means by "learn." She replies, "To do them." I ask the teacher, "Can your 'students' do the five ballet positions?" She says, "Yes, they can." I ask, "How do you know?" The students admit that they can't do all the positions because they hadn't had enough practice.

After each teacher in each group has had a chance to teach, followed by a group discussion, we meet again as a class. I ask them what insights they have gained into setting and achieving objectives and their role in the process. A lively discussion, in which the participants refer both to the various lessons they have just experienced and to their own teaching of languages, ensues.

Procedure

1. As preparation, tell the participants to create a 10-minute lesson to teach something that is *not* language. Tell them they will teach groups of a minimum of three colleagues.
2. Clarify the instructions, eliciting additional examples of what participants might teach, if necessary.
3. Have participants prepare their lessons as homework.
4. To start the activity, divide participants into groups of three or four, depending on numbers, available break-out spaces, and time.
5. Give the instructions handout. (See Handout 3.)
6. Clarify the instructions, stressing the importance of time limits and adherence to discussion questions.
7. Circulate among all the groups to ensure that participants are following instructions.
8. Stay with one group for the beginning of the discussion period to ensure that discussion is on the right track. Move to other groups during the discussion period, as feasible.
9. After each teacher in each group has completed the lesson/discussion cycle, ask participants to meet again as a large group. Conduct a discussion about what everyone has learned from the experience.

Rationale

Having teachers prepare short lessons forces them to grapple with all the issues of teaching, including what can be accomplished within a given time frame. Having them teach the lessons provides concrete instances of teaching and learning as well as shared experiences all can refer to. Focusing on something other than language allows them to approach the teaching/learning act stripped of their preconceptions and attachments to language, their usual subject matter.

Discussion questions allow participants to focus their attention and learning on the one or two aspects of teaching/learning the teacher educator wishes to address. As much can be learned from a successful lesson as from an unsuccessful one.

Caveats and Options

1. Because the Teaching Game provides concrete, shared experiences of teaching and learning, it can be used by the teacher educator to focus on any aspect of teaching and learning. My colleagues and I have used this technique, which was originally developed in U.S. Peace Corps training, with our graduate students and in teacher education workshops to have participants explore the roles of teachers and learners, the teacher's assumptions about teaching and learning, lesson planning, and the qualities of good teaching. In a seminar on teacher observation and supervision, I have used this technique as an instance of teaching, after which one of the participants, as supervisor, has a postteaching conference with the teacher.

2. Variations on the technique have included:
   a. reducing the lesson to 5 minutes instead of 10
   b. giving participants the instructions in class, and 10 minutes to prepare the lesson on the spot
   c. having a small group of participants, rather than everyone in the class, prepare lessons
   d. having one participant teach the whole class, or part of the class, while others observe, followed by discussion, which is conducted or monitored by the teacher educator.

3. Participants must have a clear idea of what is meant by "something other than language" as well as the short amount of time they will have in which to teach the lesson.

4. If the lessons are to be taught in small groups, clear instructions for the lesson and follow-up discussion are essential so that participants use their time well.
5. It is crucial for the teacher educator to circulate, both to ensure that the participants are following instructions and staying within the time limits and to help focus the discussions.
6. To ensure that the discussions stay focused and have substance, the teacher educator needs to work with each group. Participants may have difficulty giving direct feedback to a fellow participant regarding the lesson. Discussions may meander away from the discussion questions.

Handout 3

The Teaching Game

After each 10-minute lesson, please take 15 minutes to do the following. You will need a timekeeper to tell the teacher when the 10 minutes of teaching are over. Please be strict!

Teacher:
1. Tell your group what your objectives were.
2. Talk about whether you feel the objectives were achieved.
3. If so, explain how you know they were achieved. If not, talk about why you think they weren't achieved.
4. Finally, if you were to do the lesson again, is there anything you would do differently. Why?

Students:
5. Tell the teacher whether you feel you were able to achieve the objectives.
6. Tell her/him what helped you achieve them/hindered your achieving them.

Graves, K. (1993). The teaching game. In D. Freeman, with S. Cornwell (Eds.), *New ways in teacher education*. Alexandria, VA: TESOL.

Students Create Their Own Textbook for a Student Teaching Seminar

Contributor
Suzanne Irujo
Boston University,
United States

Narrative

It is midsemester, and the 12 undergraduates enrolled in my student teaching seminar are about one third of the way through their student teaching placements. They are all seniors, in their final semester of preparation as teachers of ESL, modern foreign languages, or bilingual education. The seminar is designed to provide support during student teaching as well as to develop skills in lesson planning, dealing with discipline problems, using time and space appropriately, interacting with other school personnel and with parents, and other basic issues.

As trainees come into the classroom, they turn in their student teaching journals and a written assignment. I give them a multipage handout entitled "Motivation," which they read. The handout is a synthesis of the trainees' written assignments on motivation, which they turned in the week before. With very little prompting from me, the trainees become quite involved in a discussion of various kinds of motivation, how it affects student performance, and what can be done to improve it. Personal involvement is high. It becomes obvious from the discussion that they are talking about their own and their peers' ideas. They discuss examples from their student teaching experiences, and several trainees respond to questions on the handout. When none of the trainees can answer a particular question, I make a contribution, although it may not be a completely satisfactory answer. With the comment that there are many things in teaching that do not have definitive answers, I move the class on to other activities.

Procedure

1. Select the topics to be covered during the course and arrange them in a sequence.
2. During the first class, explain that instead of reading what others have written about these topics, the trainees are going to create their own knowledge by reflecting on what they already know about teaching and then writing about and discussing it.
3. Explain the three parts of the written assignments:
   a. Trainees are to prepare a summary of what they have learned about the topic in previous education courses or from other sources.
   b. Trainees need to discuss the application to their current student teaching situation.
   c. The trainees can write about any questions they still have about the topic: things they have not learned previously or questions about how to apply what they have learned in their student teaching.
4. During the first class, model what you expect in the written assignments. Have students write about the following week's topic and collect these papers.
5. Before the next class, synthesize the written assignments into three sections: a summary of what is known, important points in application of previous knowledge to current situations, and questions.
6. Before the next class in which the topic is discussed, the trainees should try to find answers to their own questions, through teaching or talking with other teachers. They also complete a similar written assignment on the next week's topic so that the written work is ready 2 weeks ahead of each discussion.
7. The synthesis of the trainees' written work provides the basis for discussion of each week's topic. The trainees discuss unanswered questions and probe the topic from their experience.
8. Copies of the handouts are kept in a notebook, which becomes the jointly constructed text for the student teaching seminar.

Rationale

By the time undergraduate education students reach their last year, they have been exposed to a lot of information about teaching. Unfortunately, much of it is not assimilated because they are not able to relate it to their own experience. When they reach the student teaching stage, the hope is that they will remember everything they have learned and think about how to apply it. This does not happen automatically, however.

This reflection on current teaching and previous learning can be facilitated through a student teaching seminar. However, resources for doing this are not readily available. Textbooks dealing with student teaching tend to get bogged down in the minutiae of policies and procedures, and general texts on teaching simply offer more of the same things that trainees have learned for the previous 3 years. The procedure described above enables trainees to combine previously learned theory with current practice.

In this way, trainees create their own knowledge about teaching. If we give trainees a textbook about student teaching, we reinforce the idea that becoming a teacher is simply a matter of learning a body of received knowledge. If we ask them to write about their own learning and teaching, and thus to think through their belief systems, we help them become reflective teachers.

Caveats and Options

1. These procedures should be seen as guiding principles rather than as precise instructions and should be adapted as necessary to fit other situations. No procedure will work in exactly the same way every time. What is described here is the way it evolved the first time it was tried, and it will probably be very different the next time.
2. If the list of topics is developed through negotiation among the teacher educator and trainees, the seminar will be even more responsive to their needs, and they can become more aware of their own responsibility for their learning.
3. If synthesizing trainees' written assignments is too time consuming, this task could be done by the trainees themselves, on a rotating basis. Another option would be to make copies of the trainees' written assignments, instead of synthesizing them. The copies should be distributed to be read before the next class meeting.
4. This procedure assumes that the trainees are already familiar with much of the content of the course. However, it is simply a formalization of two basic premises of good learning: People learn better when new knowledge is related to what they already know; and they also learn better when learning occurs as a response to self-generated

References and Further Reading

questions. As such, it should be possible to modify it as needed and use it in any kind of learning situation.

Auerbach, E., & Wallerstein, N. (1987). *ESL for action: Problem-posing at work*. (Teachers' Guide). Reading, MA: Addison-Wesley.

Grammar Awareness

Contributor
Miriam Isaacs
Mid-Atlantic
Multifunctional
Resource Center, United
States

Narrative

This activity uses ordinary interactive communication to bring points of grammar to awareness. It can be used in the context of a grammar class or in a special unit that involves improvement of teachers' awareness of grammar.

The teacher educator has just completed a presentation on the article system in English. She now wants to give the trainees a feel for what it is like to have "real" discussions with grammatical limitations. She announces to the class, "You are going to have a conversation about what you did this weekend and what you plan to do this week. But there's a catch. You must omit all articles." Different trainees break into grins as they silently run through dialogues. The teacher educator puts the trainees into groups of three; two will talk, and one will record any lapses in the conversation.

The first trainee stumbles with "I went to the movies . . . I mean I went to movies this weekend," as the recorder notes the first error. "What was name of movie? How were reviews?" replies another trainee. "It was documentary on 1960s. Director really presented objective view of complex time." This exercise continues for several minutes so that the recorder has a turn to speak.

The point is to simulate normal discussion, while including a grammatical limitation. Thus, ordinary communication becomes extraordinary through attention to grammar, as the limitations to the participants speech impede the communication. Instead of consciously learning a form and integrating it into fluent use, the game takes the unconscious process of fluency and makes it the focus of awareness.

Procedure

1. Divide the trainees into groups of three. Two members of the triad will speak "naturally," modifying their ordinary language according to an instruction. The third keeps a record of each lapse in normal communication as the two engage in their impeded conversation.

2. The two speakers modify their language in one way only. For instance, they omit articles or they limit their speech to the past tense. Examples might include speaking only in the passive voice or having students speak without the indefinite /a/ or /an/ or the definite /the/.
3. Tally the score so that whoever makes the fewest lapses wins.
4. Rotate roles so that the monitor becomes a speaker.

Rationale

Mere presentation of a form is not sufficient to provide understanding of how the language can be influenced by its use or absence. Therefore, to develop an increased awareness of grammatical functions, teachers, whether they are to teach grammar formally or communicatively, need to be aware of English structures, the variations that are permissible, and how these variations sound and work.

The activity also breaks up the inherent dryness of formal grammar by having students manipulate grammatical structures. Teachers also need to become fully aware that grammatical categories in one language often don't exist in another or that they may appear in a very different form. Thus one outcome may be to increase teachers' understanding of the process of grammatical transfer.

Caveats and Options

1. When working with verbs, you can focus on how the auxiliary system functions by asking the paired students to speak for about 5 minutes without using any auxiliaries or modal verbs. In their conversations, they may produce language such as, "Where you eat lunch?" Students must either simplify their language or circumlocute; and at times, it sounds like "Tarzan Talk."
2. Make the students aware of the copula and the regular verbal forms of *do* and *have* in contrast to the auxiliary forms by continuing to restrict their use of the auxiliary. To modify the game, differentiate the auxiliary from the verbal functions of the verb, "I *have* a toothache and I (have) called the tooth fairy." Include the copula as auxiliary in "I *am* an angel," but not "I (am) walking to school."
3. This activity needs both preparation and resolution. It should begin with presentation and explanation of the grammatical form and its structure in English. It can then be followed by a discussion that examines the effect of that form on communication.

What I Planned—What I Did: Reflecting on Planning and Teaching During the Practicum

Contributor
Karen Johnson
The Pennsylvania State University, United States

Narrative

"I never do what is in my lesson plans," wrote a trainee during her fourth week of the practicum. "I go in with everything written out—what I'm going to do, what I want the students to do, what I hope they'll get out of the lesson, but it never ends up the way I planned."

During one of our weekly practicum meetings, five trainees sat around a table in my office discussing the problems they were having with their lesson plans. One trainee complained that she never did what was in her plans. The others agreed, stating they felt compelled to write extensive lesson plans in an attempt to anticipate what might happen during their lessons. But at the same time, they found themselves forced to shift away from what they had planned because their students responded to their instructional activities in unexpected ways. These trainees seemed to believe that if their lesson plans were not carried out, their lessons had failed.

The purpose of the following activity was to provide an opportunity for trainees to understand the relationship between the process of planning and teaching. Prior to teaching a designated lesson, I asked trainees to complete a prelesson planning guide in which they responded to specific questions related to a variety of instructional considerations (see Procedure). Immediately after teaching the lesson, I asked them to complete a postlesson planning guide in which they responded to the same instructional considerations but this time by recalling what actually happened during the lesson. I then asked them to complete a one-page written retrospective in which they focused on the differences and similarities between what they planned and what they did. They discussed their reasons for altering their planned activities, and what they might have done differently if they had the opportunity to teach the lesson again.

75

Several of the trainees agreed that by altering their planned activities they had actually taught a lesson that was much more conducive to the specific needs of their students. One trainee described deciding to skip a large-group activity on transition words in favor of a small-group activity in which the students experimented with using different transition words in their own writing. She recalled, "Once I realized that they knew these words, it made no sense to teach them, so we moved on to see if they could actually use them in their own papers." Another trainee described deciding to spend the entire class discussing two model paragraphs she had brought in on the uses of dash and colon "because the students had so many good questions and comments I thought it was more important to spend time discussing these things than doing the exercises in the book." Overall, the debriefing session became a forum for these novice teachers to understand the relationship between their own planning and teaching and, more importantly, to realize that although lesson plans are an important part of teaching, lesson plans can and should be adjusted to what actually occurs during a lesson.

Procedure

1. Prior to the lesson, have trainees write a plan in which they respond to the instructional considerations listed in Handout 4. Have them respond to each set of questions in narrative form, and list any pertinent information page numbers, time constraints, and so on about the lesson.
2. After the lesson, have trainees write a one-page retrospective in which they reflect on the differences and similarities between their planning and their teaching. Ask them to respond to the following points:
   a. Describe the most striking differences between what you planned and what you did during this lesson.
   b. Include the reasons why you altered what you had planned.
   c. If you were to have the opportunity to teach this lesson again, what would you do the same? What would you do differently?
3. Hold a debriefing session, in which pre- and postlesson planning guides are discussed. Debriefing sessions can also be held with several trainees as a forum for group discussions about the relationship between planning and teaching.

Rationale

For trainees, planning serves an important psychological need in that it helps to reduce uncertainty and enables them to maintain a sense of control over and confidence in their instructional behavior. Researchers who have examined the teachers' planning processes believe that planning is a cyclical psychological process in which teachers create a mental map that is used to guide their instructional behavior (Clark & Peterson, 1986). This map represents teachers' visualization of events that are likely to occur in the lesson, and the interaction between this mental map and what actually occurs during the lesson is an important part of teachers' decision making during classroom instruction. Conscious reflection on the relationship between planning and teaching can help trainees understand not only the role that planning plays in shaping their instructional behaviors, but also why they make "in-flight" decisions to alter their plans for valid instructional reasons. This activity should help trainees conceptualize planning as a process of constructing a flexible mental map that acts as a guide for interpreting and responding to information during classroom instruction.

Caveats and Options

1. This activity is most effective at midpoint or later in the practicum experience. Trainees need to feel comfortable with their students and their instructional placements before they can objectively reflect on discrepancies between their planning and teaching.
2. The activity is most effective when used on a sporadic basis. If it is assigned on a weekly basis, it can become a tedious task. However, when assigned every 3–4 weeks, it becomes a rich source of insight for trainees.
3. Teacher educators must be careful not to turn this activity into an evaluation of teaching ability. It is designed as an opportunity for trainees to reflect on their own instructional decision making and to articulate for themselves the relationship between their planning and teaching.

References and Further Reading

Clark, C. M., & Peterson, P. L. (1986). Teachers' thought processes. In M. C. Wittrock (Ed.), *Handbook of research on teaching* (pp. 255–296). New York: Macmillan.

Handout 4

Instructional Considerations Questionnaire

Class: Date: Teacher:

Objectives

1. What will students take away from today's lesson?
2. What skills is this an occasion to teach and how will students transfer these skills to future lessons?
3. What information should they retain from today's lesson?

Organization

1. How does this lesson follow from the previous lesson?
2. How are the skills and information in this lesson connected to tomorrow's lesson?

Motivation/Engagement

1. Why should the students care about these skills or materials?
2. How can I motivate or interest them in the material?

Scaffolding

Johnson, K. (1993). What I planned—What I did: Reflecting on planning and teaching during the practicum. In D. Freeman, with S. Cornwell (Eds.), *New ways in teacher education.* Alexandria, VA: TESOL.

1. What prior knowledge can I draw on to help explain new material?
2. How can I help students make connections between new information and prior knowledge?
3. What about today's lesson will be most difficult for students?

Presentation

1. How will I order the presentation of information?
2. How can I ensure that the students understand my directions?
3. How can I make my expectations clear to the students? Will they know what to hand in?

Assessment

1. How will I know if the students master skills and important information outlined in my objectives?
2. How will I assess their products?

Johnson, K. (1993). What I planned—What I did: Reflecting on planning and teaching during the practicum. In D. Freeman, with S. Cornwell (Eds.), *New ways in teacher education.* Alexandria, VA: TESOL.

Teacher-Initiated Solutions to Teaching Needs

Contributor
Eva Lai
The Chinese University of Hong Kong, Hong Kong

English Language Teaching meetings are organized for language teachers to identify problems they face in classroom situations and to collectively find solutions.

Narrative

Teachers are invited to a meeting through an announcement in the *Professional Teachers' Union* (PTU) *Newsletter,* which goes to all schools in Hong Kong. In the first meeting, teachers sit in small groups based on levels they teach and the type of schools they are in. They first spend 20 minutes or so writing down problems they perceive in English language teaching in their settings. Then they bring forth problems and the group tries to recommend solutions. Although the groups work by level, the problems are not restricted to that particular level, so each group gives a brief report to the whole meeting. Meanwhile all these discussions are taped for further analysis. Teachers who are interested in tackling problems then form committees to work out a detailed program to address that particular problem.

In subsequent meetings, committee members analyze problems voiced by their fellow teachers and plan for three types of activities:

- Monthly meetings on teaching methodology
- Weekly courses on English language proficiency
- Outdoor activities that are both educational and fun

These are publicized through the PTU newsletters each month to invite other interested teachers to come, thus extending interest in the group's activities. Teacher organizers feel that their professional development is enhanced because they have learned more about teaching and teacher education. Teacher participants feel they become more enthusiastic because they can meet innovative teachers from other schools.

Procedure

1. Teachers are invited to attend an organizational meeting.
2. At the first meeting, the teachers are grouped according to the level they teach. At this meeting they fill out a questionnaire that helps identify the problems they want to address (see below).

Questionnaire

List the levels you teach: For example, primary 1-3, primary 4-6

_____

Type of school: For example, government, subsidized, private

_____

Please describe as specifically as possible the greatest problem(s) with English language teaching in Hong Kong:

_____
_____
_____

In your opinion, what should be done to tackle the problem(s) mentioned above?

_____
_____
_____

---

3. After deciding on what problems or issues they will address, the teachers meet on a regular basis.

4. In subsequent meetings, they work on the issues and plan activities. The three types of activities are meetings on methodology, courses on English language proficiency, and outdoor activities.

a. Advertisement announcing monthly meetings on methodology:

A New Direction in Correcting English Compositions

- Do you often feel that, in spite of your efforts, your students show little improvement in their compositions and make the same mistakes again and again?
- And do you know that through correcting their compositions in a special way, your students can polish their English, thus reducing your heavy workload of composition correction in the long run?

---

b. Advertisement announcing an oral English proficiency course:

Oral English Proficiency Course Offered

The aim of this course is to improve teachers' oral proficiency through practice under guidance in debates, conversations, and other relevant oral activities.

TESL-trained native-English-speaking tutors will be in charge.

---

c. Advertisement announcing the English-speaking camp:

Three-Day English-Speaking Camp Begins Soon

Our 3-day camp is packed with delightful events: Talks on learning English, language games, talent show, pub tour (optional), day tour of scenic spots, etc.

All in all, there are plenty of opportunities for you to interact with native speakers, to brush up your English in a relaxed manner. So come and jon us. Booking starts on 10th January. First come, first served. Send in your cheque and mark the 3 days in your diary.

Rationale

I believe that innovations in English language teaching should come from classroom teachers because they are the frontline workers; they know what is right or wrong with the education system and can readily list the problems they face in the classroom. But as individuals, teachers may not have the energy to improve teaching singlehandedly. By inviting them to come together and voice their views, I can do a simple but effective needs analysis.

Having collected their problems, I encourage interested people to work together to address them. The problem analysis is in itself a learning process. We can look at the problems in a more detached manner. We can map the problems onto the curriculum as a whole and judge whether solutions offered are feasible or not. If we are in doubt, we can organize another seminar to get more teacher feedback.

Caveats and Options

1. It is indeed a rewarding experience to collect data from teachers and to organize activities to suit their needs. But whether we can initiate useful activities to address the problems depends very much on the ability of the organizers.

2. Having organized activities for a couple of years, I feel that it would be good to have a few applied linguists, who are not only equipped with theories but also have practical experience in the local setting, contribute to the group.
3. To successfully promote these activities, it is obvious that there must be a channel of communication among the language teachers. Having a teachers' union newsletter, as in this case, is ideal, but other forms can work as well. As long as the teachers in a certain district have a means to communicate with each other, they can invite colleagues to come for a meeting and get started.

Metalanguage Translation

Contributor
Diane Larsen-Freeman
*School for
International Training,
United States*

Narrative

I use a "translation" exercise to introduce my graduate student trainees to the metalanguage employed in my English applied linguistics course. For a few seconds on the first day of the course, I role play being a circus ringmaster. I stride to the center of the classroom and say, "Ladies and gentlemen and children of all ages. . . ." I then ask the trainees to address the question of what the ringmaster needed to know or needed to know how to do to use this greeting.

Much discussion ensues, and together we compile a list often exceeding 30 items. I "translate" each item as necessary, using the metalinguistic term we will encounter during the course. For instance, if the trainees say "vocabulary or words," I give them the term "lexicon"; if they say "plurals," I supply the term "morphemes," and so on.

Once this is done I put most of the terms into three new, untitled lists on the board. After the items have been assigned to one of these lists, I invite the trainees to offer headings for them. Together we identify the lists as those of items dealing with *form* (e.g., morphemes, syntax), *meaning* (e.g., lexicon, notions), and *use* (e.g., functions, register).

- word order — syntax
- bellowed — paralinguistics

I conclude this segment of the class by requesting that trainees select one term that is new to them and whose meaning is still unclear and to define it in their own words. I collect the definitions and then following a break, during which I have time to review the definitions, I attempt to clear up any confusion I discover in them. I also assure trainees that because this is a new language for some of them, they will have plenty of opportunity to acquire the new terms through using them in class and do not need to commit the new items to memory.

Procedure

1. Assume the role of the ringmaster and greet the audience of trainees with "Ladies and gentlemen and children of all ages. . . ."
2. Ask trainees what the ringmaster needed to know in order to be able to use this greeting. Explain that although it is a formulaic utterance, they should treat it as if it had just been created.
3. Have the trainees draw up their individual lists. After a few minutes, ask them to share their lists with a person sitting next to them and to add any new items from the other person's list to their own.
4. Compile a list with all trainee contributions on the blackboard. It is important to leave room next to each item for its "translation."
5. Returning to the beginning of the list and with a different colored piece of chalk, give the metalinguistic translation for each item when necessary. For instance, if the term on the blackboard is *word order*, write "syntax"; if the trainees note that the ringmaster *bellowed*, write "paralinguistics." For the fact that the ringmaster *stood in the middle of the classroom*, write "proxemics," etc.
6. Select from among the terms those that will be covered in the course and write each in one of three new lists. Elicit from the trainees the lists with form, meaning, and use and label each one accordingly.
7. Ask trainees to choose one new term from the three lists that they are unclear about and have them define the term as best they can on a piece of paper to be handed in. This can be done anonymously.
8. During the break, read over the definitions and identify any misunderstandings.
9. When the group has reassembled, provide any necessary clarification of terms and explain that the trainees are not expected to know the

new terms immediately, that the terms will be acquired over time with use.

Rationale

I have found that the metalanguage used in a linguistics class is often off-putting to trainees and that they are easily intimidated by the terminology. Taking a tip from Community Language Learning, I have created this introduction to the metalanguage used in my course. By treating the metalinguistic terms as the second language and the trainees' description of the ring-master's knowledge as the native language, I hope to both affirm their description and suggest that the metalanguage is simply another way of describing the same phenomenon. I explain that it is helpful to have a common language to describe language, and if we use terms the field recognizes, trainees can have access to published linguistic materials. Thus learning the terminology can be empowering, rather than intimidating.

Caveats and Options

1. This "translation exercise" would work without Step 6. I incorporate it because in subsequent analyses I will ask trainees to look at what language students will need to know about a particular structure's form, meaning, and use (Larsen-Freeman, 1991).
2. I think that this general translation approach would be suitable, no matter what the subject matter, if the initial use of terminology is potentially off-putting to trainees. Other topics might include second language acquisition (e.g., learning the nomenclature for error types—overgeneralization, negative transfer, relexification) or any of the four skills (e.g., distinguishing concepts associated with reading—skimming vs. scanning, or content vs. formal schema.)
3. To further reduce the anxiety, I suggest that as with any second language, the most enduring knowledge will likely come from using the terms. I let trainees know that they will encounter the terms again and again, and will become conversant with them in the normal course of business. I make sure that it is true that they meet the terms frequently, particularly those that have been problematic, as

evidenced by the definitions they write for the seventh step of the procedure.

References and Further Reading

Larsen-Freeman, D. (1991). Teaching grammar. In M. Celce-Murcia (Ed.), *Teaching English as a second or foreign language* (2nd ed.). Boston: Heinle and Heinle.

Correspondence Journals Between Students and Trainees

Contributor
Ilona Leki
The University of
Tennessee, United States

Narrative

About the second week of class, 15 minutes of class time are set aside for ESL students to write a brief letter of introduction to an as-yet-unknown correspondent in my ESL methodology course. The ESL students put their letters into individual folders with their names on the outside. I then distribute these folders to the trainees in my methods class. Each trainee writes a letter in response to the letter from the ESL students and adds that letter to the one already in the folder, writing their own name on the outside as well for ease in distribution each week. The trainees are instructed not to correct anything their ESL correspondents write, but rather to respond naturally as they would to any letter. These folders are then redistributed to the original ESL authors and the ESL students reply to their correspondents.

The letter writing continues back and forth between the two classes once a week for about 10 weeks with each pair of correspondents writing on any topic of interest to them. About 20 minutes of class time is set aside once a week for the members of each class to read the letter addressed to them for that week and to respond to it. All the writing is done in class; neither group of students may take a folder home. The teacher educator's responsibility is merely to distribute the folders to the students in both classes. Occasionally, the ESL students and the trainees read and respond to their weekly letters on their own.

At the end of the 10-week period, participants from both classes are invited to a pot-luck meet-your-correspondent party at my home. Here they meet for the first time the person to whom they have been writing all semester. Often phone numbers are exchanged and the U.S. trainees and the international ESL students continue their budding friendships outside of class.

Procedure

1. Have each language student write a letter of introduction to a trainee. Each student puts the letter into a folder and writes his/her name on the outside.
2. Distribute the folders to trainees. Each trainee responds to a letter and puts the letter into the folder along with that of the correspondent. The trainees put their names on the outside of their folders.
3. The following week, redistribute the folders to the original language student authors for their responses.
4. Continue the letter writing back and forth for about 10 weeks.
5. Introduce the pairs of correspondents for the first time at a social event organized for that purpose.

Rationale

This technique is intended to benefit both language students and trainees. The students have an opportunity to engage in writing addressed to a real audience. Their correspondents are generally native speakers of English and particularly interested in language students. The student's writing is not corrected so as not to stifle the development of writing fluency. The writing is not an extra burden because it is done in class with the classroom teacher's support if necessary and is not evaluated in any way. The trainees benefit from having the opportunity to see what second language writing looks like and to learn directly from their correspondents about the life of a student.

Caveats and Options

1. Correspondence journals can be used with nearly any level of ESL student beyond absolute beginners (e.g., Peyton & Reed, 1990). Correspondents often exchange little gifts during the correspondence as well, attaching them to the inside of the folder.
2. If the number of students is greater than the number of trainees, trainees can be assigned two correspondents. If the number of trainees is greater, more than one can correspond with just one student.
3. Usually the correspondence is quite lively, with students requesting either more class time to complete their weekly letter or permission to take the folder home. Taking the folder home is not a good idea

because, despite the best of intentions, people forget to bring it, and then the forgetful person's correspondent is disappointed to receive no letter that week. When a student from either class is absent, I simply write a note to the correspondent saying that their partner did not come to class that day, sometimes adding a further word.

4. Very occasionally the correspondents get into a rut and can't seem to find anything to say to each other. I place the burden of carrying on the conversation on the trainees. I may try to help by suggesting a topic for them to explore with their correspondent or other members of the class may do so. In their letters these students are free to ask their correspondents questions about the United States, the university, English, or any topic of interest to them in a nonthreatening environment.

5. This technique has also been used with success between ESL students and native-English-speaking students in freshman composition classes.

6. It makes no difference whether the teacher educator and the teacher of the ESL class are the same or different people. No extra work is created either for the teachers of the language or the teacher education class. Furthermore, both groups of students take a great deal of pleasure in the technique, in the mystery of not knowing their correspondent, and in the excitement of finally meeting the correspondent socially.

Acknowledgment

I would like to credit Teresa Dalle of Memphis State University with having originated this activity.

References and Further Reading

Peyton, J. K., & Reed, L. (1990). *Dialogue journal writing with nonnative English speakers: A handbook for teachers.* Alexandria, VA: TESOL.

Face-to-Face: Experiences in Cultural Adjustment

Contributor
Nancy Lee Lucas
*Broward County
(Florida) School Board,
United States*

Narrative

The teacher educator, Anne, is working with a group of 20 participants. This segment of the workshop deals with cultural adjustment. Anne directs the participants to stand up and find a partner. She tells them to take 30 seconds to look at one another very closely and then turn back-to-back. When the participants are back-to-back, she instructs them to make one physical change, turn back around, and identify these changes to one another. Amidst many smiles, some participants take off glasses or remove ties; others take off watches or rings.

After about 30 seconds, the participants are directed to stand back-to-back again. With a straight face, Anne tells them they now have 20 seconds to make 20 physical changes. Anne waits; there are strong reactions from the participants: "You've got to be kidding;" "Impossible!" Anne also sees stunned looks on some participants' faces. Some people do attempt to make 20 physical changes in 20 seconds but find it a nearly impossible task. When Anne notices a general sense of frustration in the group, she announces to the participants in mock disgust, "Never mind. You can all sit down." A debriefing period now begins as Anne asks, "How did you feel when you were asked to make one physical change?" There are comments such as "It was easy," "No problem," or "I had fun." She then asks participants, "How did you feel when I asked you to make 20 physical changes?" "It all seemed very frustrating"; "I was nervous"; "It made me angry"; "I was confused"; "I felt overwhelmed."

Anne then asks, "Why did you feel the way you did when I asked you to make one physical change?" One person says, "I didn't have to make much of a change, I didn't have to think very much to make it." Anne then follows with "Why did you feel the way you did when I asked you to make

20 physical changes?" The participants respond that they did not have time to make all those changes, they did not know what changes to make, or they liked themselves the way they were, and automatically resisted the change.

Anne introduces the concept of cultural adjustment and the stages of cultural assimilation and discusses them with the group. She provides closure by eliciting anecdotal real-life experiences from the participants and adding when necessary to illustrate each of the steps.

Procedure

1. Get an overhead projector or prepare a handout on steps to cultural adjustment and assimilation; also have newsprint, an easel, markers, or a chalkboard to record participants' feelings. You will need seating that is flexible and allows enough room to stand in pairs.
2. Direct the participants to stand in pairs face-to-face, look carefully at one another, turn back-to-back, make one physical change, turn again face-to-face, and identify the change each other has made.
3. Direct the participants to again turn back-to-back and make 20 physical changes.
4. Have participants compare their reactions to Steps 2 and 3.
5. Compare the participants' comments to the steps of cultural adjustment and assimilation and share the list of steps to cultural assimilation (Gochenour & Janeway, 1993).
6. Elicit specific examples from the participants and add anecdotes when necessary to illustrate each step.

Rationale

Teaching culture can be a difficult task in teacher education programs. What can the teacher educator do to convey important aspects of cultural adjustment as it relates to language students in nonthreatening and enjoyable ways? This activity provides the opportunity to "experience" some of these effects in a simulated fashion. Once participants experience how it feels to find themselves face-to-face with a new culture, they tend to better identify the cultural differences experienced by students and also to attach feelings to these cultural contrasts. Each new conflicting value or behavior now represents for the participants a serious struggle to assimilate.

Caveats and Options

1. The individual sections of the technique must move quickly in order for the activity to have the most impact. A good rule of thumb is to use a 30-second time limit for the participants to respond to each set of directions. Be sure to allow time, however, for the group to laugh, talk, and settle down after each section of the activity. Also be sure to wait just long enough to get the desired reactions from the participants—disgust, shock, disbelief, confusion—before moving on to the next step of this activity.
2. It is a good idea to emphasize that the steps to cultural adjustment do not happen sequentially. As you introduce the stages of cultural

adjustment to the group, personal anecdotes to illustrate each step should be shared.

3. This face-to-face training activity provides an informative and enjoyable way for the teacher educator to elicit feelings and aspects of cultural adjustment and assimilation to teachers of all subject areas. A plus to this strategy is that it requires little preparation and few materials to successfully implement. The activity can also be used with small or large groups, from 2 people to 60.

4. This activity takes anywhere from 20 minutes to an hour, depending on the amount of debriefing and/or discussion elicited from the group and the number of specific examples used to illustrate the steps to cultural assimilation. The identification of these stages with correlating examples provides effective closure to this training experience.

5. The activity can be embedded between a short presentation of multicultural demographics and facts at national, state, and local levels and discussion of specific cultural differences between the U.S. school culture and the cultures our language minority students represent.

6. A comparison of the first few days on a new job with an aspect of cultural assimilation may be discussed for those participants who have not personally experienced culture shock.

7. The activity can be used to stimulate a discussion of change—in organizations, workplaces, school environments, or policies. By asking how many participants initially resisted the activity, how many made changes by *taking away* something, and how many participants thought of *rearranging* or *adding* something, the teacher educator can focus the follow-up discussion on how people view change.

References and Further Reading

Gochenour, T., & Janeway, A. (1993). Seven concepts in cross-cultural interaction. In T. Gochenour (Ed.), *Beyond experience.* Yarmouth, ME: Intercultural Press.

Saville-Troike, M. (1976). *Foundation of English as a second language: Theory and method for multicultural education.* Englewood Cliffs, NJ: Prentice Hall.

Seelye, H. N. (1981). *Teaching culture: Strategies for foreign-language education.* Skokie, IL: National Textbook Co.

Self-Observation in Teacher Education

Contributor
Magali de Moraes Menti
*Centro de Ensino e
Pesquisa da Língua
Inglesa, Brazil*

This activity is used in the teacher training course held at our school every semester. The course serves as a refresher for in-service teachers or as preservice training for individuals who wish to teach at the school. The course includes 45 hours of input, 12 hours of classroom observation, and 12 hours of teaching practice with a group of students brought together for this purpose. The activity is used to provide teachers and trainees with the opportunity for self-initiated, self-directed, and self-observed growth.

Narrative

It is Monday, Veronica's day to be observed. The video camera is set up and has been tested. Veronica meets with her supervisor, and they discuss the content of the class and the techniques Veronica will use. Veronica also uses the time to get some last-minute advice and tips.

Veronica teaches her class, which goes well. After the class she takes the videotape home to view it prior to her follow-up discussion with her supervisor. The follow-up discussion takes place only after Veronica has watched the recording of her class and has had time to go over the following list of things to ponder while watching the video:

1. Search for positive moments and behavior in the lesson.
2. Choose one aspect to be improved next class and consider how this could be done.
3. Give yourself a grade from 1 to 10 on the lesson as a whole.
4. Look at your interaction with the class and students' interaction with each other.
5. Contrast how you felt during the class and how you appeared to feel.
6. Contrast the impression you had of your class right after it was taught and now as you review it.
7. What has improved in your teaching since your last class.

8. Choose one aspect of the class you want to research or get second opinions on.
9. Look for examples of what your supervisor has said about your teaching.

Following her supervisor's suggestion, Veronica watches the tape twice: once to satisfy her curiosity and then to focus on the list. She then schedules a meeting with her supervisor to discuss her teaching and any discoveries she has made; the supervisor's role is to offer guidance and encourage sharing of experiences.

Both discussion meetings are held with only Veronica and her supervisor; however, other members of the class may participate at Veronica's invitation. The objective of the taping is to provide the trainees with information about their own classes—which they may decide to keep to themselves and process alone. The follow-up discussions aim at helping Veronica discover more about her teaching practice and thus improve it. They do not in any way aim at assessment of her classes.

Procedure

1. Apprise the trainees of the class taping. Make the objectives clear and teach the trainees to handle the video camera themselves.
2. Have the trainees prepare their classes with the aid of their peers and supervisor.
3. Have a preobservation discussion with each trainee during which last-minute details are set and doubts clarified.
4. The trainee sets up the camera, which is equipped with wide-angle lens to permit ample coverage of class. The camera should be aimed at the trainee, the blackboard, and as many students as possible. The class is taped.
5. Afterwards, the trainee watches the tape alone and goes over the list of things to ponder while watching the video (see Handout 5).
6. Afterwards, schedule a follow-up meeting with the trainee.
7. Let the trainee lead the meeting, discussing all or only some of the topics of the list with you in the role of listener and advisor.

Rationale

The aim of this technique is to enable trainees to pursue self-initiated, self-directed, and self-observed growth. In self-directed development, one gathers data about one's own performance or behavior. Such growth springs from a trained critical eye, one that is able to criticize, either positively or negatively, one's own work. Work one starts by oneself, driven by one's own will to improve, tends to have a stronger effect and be more long lasting. These data are dealt with, processed, stored, or modified as experience and knowledge about oneself.

Caveats and Options

1. Trainees take some time to truly grasp the objective of this activity. Stress for them the importance of self-observation and self-development.
2. The tendency. is to depend on the teacher educator—having the teacher educator watch all the recordings or go over all the details on the list, searching for approval. This should be dealt with patiently until it disappears. Once this tendency abates, it will surely serve to strengthen trainees' confidence in their work.

3. Trainees may have their peers watch their recordings if they want second opinions and/or to share experiences. The follow-up discussions may also take place with the presence of peers or during the class for the same reasons. However, if trainees choose to do either, it should be made clear that this is optional.

4. Teacher educators must not take command of the discussions or watch the recordings with the trainees on a regular basis; doing so will encourage the trainees' dependency on their view of teaching.

Handout 5

List of Things to Ponder While Watching Your Video

1. Search for positive moments and behavior in the lesson.
2. Choose one aspect to be improved on next class and consider how this could be done.
3. Give yourself a grade from 1 to 10 on the lesson as a whole.
4. Look at your interaction with the class and students' interaction with each other.
5. Contrast how you felt during the class and how you appeared to feel.
6. Contrast the impression you had of your class right after it was taught and now as you view it.
7. What has improved in your teaching since your last class?
8. Choose one aspect of the class you want to research or get second opinions on.
9. Look for examples of what your supervisor has said about your teaching.

Menti, M. (1993). Self-observation in teacher education. In D. Freeman, with S. Cornwell (Eds.), *New ways in teacher education*. Alexandria, VA: TESOL.

Textbook Evaluation:
The Anatomy of a Textbook

Contributor
Joan Morley
The University of Michigan, United States

Narrative

The teacher educator, Ellen, assembles a Book Fair in which 150–200 ESL textbooks are chosen and put on open-access display. The books are grouped into as many categories as may be useful: level of difficulty; general versus specific content; appropriateness for elementary, middle school, secondary, college, and adult students; skill areas (i.e., listening, speaking, reading, writing); linguistic categories (e.g., grammar, pronunciation, vocabulary); specialties (e.g., singing, poetry, jazz chants).

In preparation for a homework assignment, Ellen distributes and discusses the text evaluation questionnaire, explaining items and answering questions. Two sample text analyses are then distributed for homework study.

In the next class, trainees work in pairs or groups of threes, browsing through the book fair to select a book to be reviewed using the text evaluation questionnaire. Working together, they prepare a two-page report. These reports are then typed and distributed to all participants. Peer comments and suggestions are invited, and these are given in writing directly to the authors of the report. The original reports are then revised and submitted for inclusion in the class collection that will be prepared and distributed at the end of the course.

Finally, Ellen prepares copies of the class collection for distribution to all class members or participants. The trainees have not only participated in a valuable hands-on learning experience but have developed a useful tangible reference to add to their professional library.

Procedure

1. Prior to the class, arrange for a large number of ESL textbooks to be put on display; the more books, the better.

2. As the trainees arrive, hand out the text evaluation questionnaire.
3. Ask the trainees to work in groups to select one text to review.
4. In their group, the trainees prepare a two-page report following the textbook evaluation questionnaire (see Handout 6).
5. Give copies of the reports to all class members. After they make comments and suggestions in writing, return the reports to the authors.
6. After the groups incorporate the suggestions, prepare a copy of all reports for distribution to the class.

Rationale

The variety of ESL/EFL textbooks available from book publishers today is overwhelming. Criteria for choosing textbooks depend on numerous factors, some of which involve the overall curriculum planning for any given course as well as for the sequence of courses in a particular program.

Novice and experienced teachers, as well as students in graduate TESL programs, find participation in hands-on text evaluation tasks useful and challenging. Also, materials selection is a collaborative process in many teaching situations. The emphasis on group work in evaluating textbooks can help trainees gain a sense of the process.

Caveats and Options

1. I have used this activity in both teacher training courses and in-service training workshops. In the latter, time to revise reports may be limited, however. In that case, it is also possible to use Steps 1–4 only.
2. Sociopolitical issues such as gender roles, portrayal of cultural values, and representation of dominant and minority cultures can be added as categories to the questionnaire.

References and Further Reading

Canale, M., & Swain, M. (1980). Theoretical bases of communicative approaches to second language teaching and testing. *Applied Linguistics, 1,* 1–47.

Dubin, F. (1983). *Teacher/learner interaction series.* (Video Cassette and Teacher Manual). Los Angeles: University of Southern California.

Wright, T. (1987). *The roles of teachers and learners.* Oxford: Oxford University Press.

Handout 6

Text Evaluation Questionnaire

Prepare a two-page summary description of the textbook and any supplementary tapes or workbooks in the following nine areas. The task is to do a critical description of the text; you are to analyze how it is put together. The reporting notes should be short, but comprehensive. Use a phrase outline, notes, or whatever is most appropriate for you and your chosen text.

1. Identifying information
   List the following identifying information:
   - Name of the text
   - Author(s)
   - Date of publication
   - Name of publisher and city of publication
   - Price
   - Audience for whom text appears to be intended (age of learners, level of proficiency, purposes for studying English)
   - Components (books, tapes, answer keys, scripts).
2. Author beliefs about theory and practice in language learning and teaching
   a. Make brief statements.
   b. Cite place(s) in the text where this information is discussed.
      Note. The essentials of the author's belief system may not be explicit; in some cases statements may be misleading. It is often necessary to glean this information from presentations in the text.
3. Language content
   a. Describe the predominant types of texts, exercises, activities, and tasks in the book.

Morley, J. (1993). Textbook evaluation: The anatomy of a textbook. In D. Freeman, with S. Cornwell (Eds.), *New ways in teacher education.* Alexandria, VA: TESOL.

b. Evaluate the realistic nature—authentic, well-simulated, contrived—of the materials, activities, etc.

4. Learner's role, tasks, goals
   a. Describe what the learners are to do with the materials and the ways they are to manipulate the content, to complete the activity or task or exercise.
   b. Assess the learner goals of the materials in terms of how they will advance the learner's communicative competencies: linguistic, sociolinguistic, discourse, strategic (Canale & Swain, 1980).

5. Teacher's role
   a. Describe what the teacher is to do with the material to facilitate learning.
   b. Describe the teacher's roles in terms of master controller, manager, participant, and observer (Dubin, 1983; see also Wright, 1987).

6. Assessment of language learning
   a. Describe how the text assesses the learner's movement or goals.

7. Potential for engagement of the learner with the materials
   a. Note the potential for interest, appeal, and satisfaction with the use of materials.
   b. Note the degrees of relevance, transferability, and task orientation for maximum learner involvement.

8. Summary notes of the major strengths of the text

9. Summary notes of the major weaknesses of the text

Morley, J. (1993). Textbook evaluation: The anatomy of a textbook. In D. Freeman, with S. Cornwell (Eds.), *New ways in teacher education.* Alexandria, VA: TESOL.

Facilitating Seminar Discussions With a "Designated Reader"

Contributor
John M. Murphy
Georgia State University, United States

Narrative

In a graduate seminar, trainees are seated in a large circle. Once everyone settles down and the teacher educator has finished with a few procedural announcements, he turns responsibilities for leading the seminar discussion over to one of the trainees. Elaine, the session's Designated Reader, begins by distributing a handout that outlines the major themes in a reading that everyone has prepared for today's class. The reading, from Allwright and Bailey (1991), is devoted to the topic of input and interaction in second language classrooms.

Elaine says, "Just to get started, why don't you take a few minutes to review the major themes presented in the reading with someone sitting next to you. What are some of the more important issues that Allwright and Bailey are introducing?" The trainees begin to do as requested, working together in groups of two. Some compare the chapter headings with Elaine's handout; others move directly to the discussion questions at the end of the chapter; two trainees are trying to interpret a figure in the reading, while others have begun to examine one of the chapter's classroom transcripts.

After about 8 minutes have passed, Elaine calls for everyone's attention. She then explains that she is going to take about 15 minutes to go over what she considers the main points in the reading. Then, with her handout and the open text, she begins to orally outline the chapter's major themes.

While Elaine reviews the topics, she is interrupted occasionally by other members of the class and, less often, by the teacher educator. Some trainees introduce their own examples that seem relevant to the topics under discussion. Several trainees ask questions that prompt further comments from classmates. The teacher educator takes part in a few of these exchanges as well.

Procedure

1. As the Designated Reader, the trainee is responsible for taking the seminar participants through the reading selection that everyone has prepared for the day's class. He or she leads the discussion.
2. The Designated Reader's role is to represent the author's voice in the discussion. Because this is essentially a text-based summary and review, the Designated Reader is encouraged to leave the conceptually driven analyses and interpretive responses to the other members of the class.
3. Although the Designated Reader takes primary responsibility for the summary/review, other members of the class are encouraged to assist.
4. In preparation, the Designated Reader should read the assigned selection several different times; highlight the author's salient points; scribble notes, questions, and brief responses directly in the margins of the text; and take time to reflect, synthesize, and think over the reading.
5. After leading everyone through the assigned text, the Designated Reader is welcome to voice reservations about the content. However, these more interpretive responses should come after everyone has developed a fuller understanding and appreciation of the reading.

Rationale

The activity is based on the idea that seminar discussions of readings should be interactive processes that encompass elements of both bottom-up and top-down interpretation. It also places responsibility for leading seminar discussions upon the shoulders of preservice trainees. The challenge is to help ensure that major concepts from a specified reading are, in fact, being incorporated into seminar discussions. So the Designated Reader is asked to contribute from a bottom-up, textually driven point of view. To complement this effort, everyone else is encouraged to interact with, respond to, question, draw connections to, and debate the meaning of the assigned reading. By taking responsibility for weaving the author's ideas into the seminar discussion, the Designated Reader is free to leave more interpretive responses to everyone else. The format helps to ensure that discussions are interactive, while maintaining the anchor of one reader's text-based contributions.

Caveats and Options

1. The activity can place pressure upon trainees who feel constrained by representing someone else's ideas.
2. Some trainees prefer to lead discussions in a conventional manner. Others prefer written discussion guides, interactive games, in-class debates, demonstrations, microteaching, and panel discussions (see Ellis, 1990).
3. It is helpful to discuss the rationale for this activity. One alternative is to present the activity as an option that will be explored during the first few weeks of the course. In this way, if trainees become uncomfortable with it, there is time to address their reservations and to try other means for facilitating interactive seminar discussions.

References and Further Reading

Allwright, D., & Bailey, K. M. (1991). *Focus on the language classroom: An introduction to classroom research for language teachers*. New York: Cambridge University Press.

Ellis, R. (1990). Activities and procedures for teacher preparation. In J. C. Richards & D. Nunan (Eds.), *Second language teacher education* (pp. 26–36). New York: Cambridge University Press.

Introducing Trainees to the Topic of Lesson Planning

Contributor
John M. Murphy
*Georgia State
University, United
States*

Narrative

The teacher educator, Dr. Hemingway, begins the day's activities by displaying an overhead projection:

An Example of a Second Language Lesson Plan Format

Teacher's Name _____ Date of Lesson _____

Estimated Time of the Lesson (or activity)

1. Teaching Point Highlighted _____
   _____

2. Preassessment Activity _____

3. Relationship to Current Unit _____

4. Pre-entry Performance _____

5. Performance Objectives _____

6. Criterion Level _____

7. Materials/Resources _____

8. Procedures (Student/Classroom Activities) _____

Step 1: Introduction (Time:) Step n: Concluding activity that permits informal assessment of criterion level established (see No. 6, above)

   _____

9. Assignment (optional) _____

   _____

10. Contingency Plans

   _____

Comments/Self-Evaluation (Fill out after lesson is taught)

Adapted from Celce-Murcia & Gorman (1986, p. 297).

He says, "As you can see, this is a sample format for creating a lesson plan. You will be trying to match brief written definitions and examples of each component with the 10 numbered headings on the overhead."

Dr. Hemingway explains that the planned activity will be an adaptation of the "strip paragraph" procedure discussed in their course readings. The trainees then arrange themselves into small groups, and Dr. Hemingway distributes a set of 10 paper strips to each group. These strips contain the definitions and examples of the components listed on the overhead. The definitions and examples, four to six sentences each, are presented on separate strips of paper. Dr. Hemingway says, "You have all the information you will need in order to match these paragraphs with the corresponding headings on the lesson plan on the overhead. Your task is to work collaboratively and to share information as you try to match each of the paragraphs with its appropriate heading." The trainees begin to read the paper strips, and eventually start describing, comparing, and discussing the information presented. Dr. Hemingway lends assistance as needed.

After about 15 minutes, all of the groups have completed the initial stage of the task. He then asks everyone to rearrange themselves into dyads to begin working with a new partner from another group. Their task is to compare notes and agree on their identifications of the 10 descriptors. After a few more minutes, many trainees begin to ask for clarifications about various components of a lesson plan. Dr. Hemingway fields their questions, discusses the format and function of the lesson plan, elaborates on the meaning of the written descriptors, and provides additional examples. The class ends in a whole-group discussion about the role and purpose of lesson planning.

Procedure

1. Reproduce copies of a lesson plan scheme adapted from teacher reference resources such as Celce-Murcia & Gorman (1986) or Harmer (1991), including an overhead transparency and corresponding sets of strip paragraphs that are based upon the prose discussions and examples in these texts.
2. Project the lesson-plan scheme on an overhead.
3. Discuss with trainees the potential importance of lesson planning.
4. Briefly discuss the rationale for the experiential nature of the activity.

5. Have the group review the steps of a "strip paragraph" activity (see Klippel, 1987, p. 47).
6. Divide trainees into small groups of three or four.
7. Hand out one complete set of the 10 strip paragraphs to each group. The sets of strip paragraphs present definitions and examples of the various components of the lesson plan, with headings omitted. The trainees in each group begin to take turns reading the 10 strip paragraphs. After everyone has read, the trainees exchange information and they try to match each of the paragraphs with one of the components of the scheme on the overhead projection.
8. Once the small groups have completed this step, ask everyone to rearrange themselves into dyads to work with a new partner from another group. Ask the dyads to compare notes and continue their discussion. Lend assistance as needed.

Rationale

Lesson planning is a topic of sometimes heated debate. Administrators, parents, and adult students assume that a teacher should be able to compose written plans for classroom instruction on a regular basis. Many teachers depend upon such plans in order to help structure a priori what they plan to do with groups of learners. Further, one of the first things many supervisors request prior to a formal classroom observation is a copy of the teacher's lesson plan.

In addition, this activity models a popular instructional procedure while covering content of a teacher education course. Day (1990) distinguishes between action-system and subject-matter knowledge and argues that the development of both areas is essential to the preparation of teachers. Thus, this activity is an opportunity to acquire action-system knowledge—the strip paragraph activity—through firsthand experience, while incorporating the subject-matter knowledge of lesson planning.

References and Further Reading

Celce-Murcia, M., & Gorman, T. (1986). Preparing lesson-plans. In M. Celce-Murcia & L. McIntosh (Eds.), *Teaching English as a second or foreign language* (pp. 295–301). Rowley, MA: Newbury House.

Day, R. (1990). Teacher observation in second language teacher education. In J. C. Richards & D. Nunan (Eds.), *Second language teacher education* (pp. 43–61). New York: Cambridge University Press.

Harmer, J. (1991). *The practice of English language teaching*. New York: Longman.

Klippel, F. (1987). *Keep talking: Communicative fluency activities for language teaching*. New York: Cambridge University Press.

Program Evaluation:
A Simulation

Contributor
Denise E. Murray
*San José State
University, United
States*

Narrative

A class of 17 graduate trainees in an MA TESOL program are given a handout with the information presented below. I divide the class into four groups by having trainees count off by four. I distribute the task and explain that the situation is one in which I am currently involved.

1. An ESL program at a community college has asked you to be a consultant on a grant to evaluate their program. As part of the grant proposal, they need a proposal from you, describing the procedures you would use for such an evaluation. Prepare an outline of the proposal for evaluating the program.

2. Choose one person to present your outline to the class. Each presentation is limited to 5 minutes. The class will then have the opportunity to ask questions of the proposer.

3. The class will assume it is a community college committee and vote on which proposal to accept. Be prepared to argue for/against particular proposals. As you question and vote, think about how well the proposal covers all aspects of the program and how appropriate the evaluation methods are.

I wrote such a proposal, which was accepted by the community college, and I am now involved in the program evaluation. I explain that trainees may be asked to do similar evaluations, for example, a self-study of a program in which they might teach in the future. I then explain the steps of the task.

In their groups, trainees are to develop an evaluation proposal. I circulate and provide information as needed, but do not clarify what should or should not be part of an evaluation process.

One member from each group presents the outline of their proposal for the evaluation process. At the end of each presentation, class members ask questions. The four proposals are different. The first one focuses on what constitutes a good program, talking about what should or should not be in the program; the next three recommend a needs analysis, using a survey form; the final one recommends a survey of faculty and the community as well as of the students. The surveys all ask about student backgrounds, goals for being in the course, and future uses of English. One proposal suggests observation of representative classes at each language level. Another suggests pre- and posttesting of students to measure their growth. Another suggests a 3-year plan that examines retention and student success. Yet another suggests surveying other courses at the college to determine how successful the ESL students are in those classes. All suggest collecting current curricula guides and course outlines.

As the class member describes the group's evaluation procedure, others ask questions: "Why use a survey?" "How will they find out exactly what the program is like, if you can not rely on curricula guides and course outlines?" "How will they survey the community and alumni?"

The class then discusses the pros and cons of each program, as though they were members of the community college committee that will decide which proposal to accept. After the discussion, the "committee" votes. The majority want the proposal that includes faculty, student, and alumni surveys; observations of actual classrooms; and collection of curricula guides, course outlines, and trainee work. A couple of trainees feel wedded to their own proposal and vote for it despite the negative comments from other class members.

I then talk about which model I would have voted for and why, and also describe the evaluation model I am currently using in my grant. The class is delighted that I agree with the majority and that my own accepted evaluation plan is very similar to their first choice.

Procedure

1. Give trainees the task (see Handout 7), which they will work in groups to develop.
2. Tell trainees they will make a 5-minute presentation, followed by 5 minutes of questions clarifying the proposal. They are to present their proposal as a committee, and to field questions collectively. The aim is to convince the class of the benefit of their proposal.
3. Allow about 10 minutes for general discussion, during which the class selects once proposal. Tell the class they are to function as the board of the community college.

Rationale

I use this simulation in a graduate class in testing, evaluation, and research. The class has already explored assessment of students; this simulation helps them think through how to assess a program. I use a simulation rather than lecture/discussion because they already know the fundamental principles and procedures for assessing language, and the situation simulates a project in which I am currently involved. As a result, they can bring their own knowledge to bear on a real-world problem. I believe it works for precisely these reasons—trainees have the background knowledge and the situation is real.

Caveats and Options

1. Trainees need some background in TESOL methods and testing before they can fruitfully gain from this exercise.
2. It is also best done later in the semester after several other group activities have built up trust among all trainees. Without that trust, trainees are not willing to comment on each other's proposals and, even more importantly, as happened in the lesson described, will cling to their own proposals, even when faced with a clearly more appropriate model.
3. In a class with more time, the groups can present their proposals in writing and have all trainees evaluate each one independently before the committee presentation and question time. This allows trainees to think through some of the issues in more depth.

Handout 7

Program Evaluation Simulation

1. Work in groups to develop the following task:
   An ESL program at a community college has asked you to be a consultant on a grant to evaluate their program. As part of the grant proposal, they need a proposal from you, describing the procedures you would use for such an evaluation. Prepare an outline of the proposal for evaluating the program.
2. Prepare a 5-minute presentation, to be followed by 5 minutes of questions clarifying the proposal. You will choose one person to present your outline to the class. Each presentation is limited to 5 minutes. The class will then have the opportunity to ask questions of the proposer.
3. There will be a 10-minute general discussion. The class will assume it is a community college committee and vote on which proposal to accept. Be prepared to argue for/against particular proposals. As you question and vote, think about how well the proposal covers all aspects of the program and how appropriate the evaluation methods are.

Murray, D. E. (1993). Program evaluation: A simulation. In D. Freeman, with S. Cornwell (Eds.), *New ways in teacher education* Alexandria, VA: TESOL.

Creating Seminar Groups in Large Graduate Classes

Contributor
Gayle Nelson
*Georgia State
University, United
States*

Narrative

The following description is from a graduate course in approaches to teaching ESL/EFL. The trainees have read Richards and Rodgers' (1987) chapter, "Method, Approach, Design, and Procedure." At the beginning of the class, the 24 TESL graduate trainees almost fill the university classroom. The teacher educator collects group plans from the three trainees who are in charge of their groups on this particular day.

Trainees break into their groups and each group goes to a different room. As unobtrusively as possible, the teacher educator observes one of the three groups, sitting on the outside of the circle, listening to the interactions, and writing first person comments on the facilitator's plan: "As I read over your plan, I notice that you have hit on the main points of the chapter;" or "I feel like the group is enjoying this; they seem focused and involved!" After about 10 minutes, the teacher educator leaves to observe one of the other groups.

As she walks into the second room, eight trainees are sitting at desks in a closely knit circle with notebooks and books open on their desks. Don McKay, the group facilitator, is leaning forward. He has distributed his plan to the other trainees and is explaining what he would like the others to do. The portion of the plan he is talking about follows.

He says, referring to Part 2 of the plan, "I'd like you to associate the jumbled words with the heading. I mean, do objectives come out of approach, design, or procedure?" One trainee says, "I associate objectives more with design," but others disagree. They continue to state and support

116

Portion of A Facilitator's Group Plan

Part 2—The second objective: Discuss the different components of a method. Put the jumbled words under the heading you think they are most related to.

APPROACH   DESIGN   PROCEDURE

objectives   drills   beliefs   activities   structuralism
materials   language theory   tactics   behaviorism
theory   syllabus   roles   content   principles   assumptions
organization   mentalism   form   resources   learning theory

1. Let's come up with some simple definitions for approach, design, and procedure (i.e., An approach is.... A design is.... A procedure is....).
2. Is a syllabus the same thing as a method?
3. Can different methods use the same procedure? If so, then where is the difference between two methods that use the same procedure?

their points of view. One trainee looks at the chapter for evidence to support his view. Don says, "There's no right or wrong answer, just give your opinion." As he senses that the discussion is winding down, he offers another term and asks trainees if they would put it under approach, design, or procedure.

After they have discussed all of the words listed, Don says, "Okay, now let's come up with some simple definitions for approach, design, and procedure. What's an approach?" One trainee says, "What you believe," and another says "Your assumptions." Later, Don prompts by saying, "Design." One trainee says, "Layout," and another says, "Organization." Other responses include, "Content, what you're going to teach, how you get to the end, your strategy, and the relationship between design and procedure." The discussion continues as the teacher educator leaves the room.

Procedure

1. At the beginning of the term, distribute the course syllabus, which includes the following:

   Group Facilitators: Group facilitators choose the focus and organization of the group. On the day you are responsible for your group, you need to give me a one- to two-page plan. The plan should give me an idea of how you're structuring the group (e.g., asking questions, having participants complete an exercise) and the major points to be covered by the group. Please do not ask questions to test your peers' recall of the articles. Instead, focus on students *exploring* the issues raised by the readings. Plan for a 30-minute discussion for each reading. A sample plan is attached.

2. Bring in a list of course readings (articles, chapters, and books) and the dates they will be discussed.

3. Ask trainees to sign up for specific course readings or chapters that they will be responsible for.

4. Ask all trainees to read the assigned readings for the given class and come to class prepared to talk.

5. The trainee facilitators read the article or chapter and create a plan for structuring their group.

6. At the beginning of the class, the trainee facilitators give their plans to the teacher educator.

7. Trainees break into their groups and begin the discussion.

8. Move from room to room, listening to parts of all the discussions and writing comments on the facilitator's plan.

9. When the groups have finished their discussions, trainees return to the classroom. Return the plans with comments on them to the facilitators.

Rationale

Stevick (1980) suggests that if students invest in a class, they learn more than if they don't. He defines investment as making a commitment or a choice. In this procedure, the trainee facilitators have a personal stake in what happens. Also trainees are more likely to talk about and, therefore, to invest in both the content of the readings and the successful functioning of their group if a teacher educator does not participate in the interactions. The trainee cannot assume that the teacher educator will assume the usual role of controlling the discussion.

The facilitator enters the course readings at a level of understanding that makes sense to the trainees as peers. By connecting the content of the readings to what their peers already know, the facilitators and other trainees will likely remember more of what they have read. Trainees also seem to develop a sense of responsibility for the continued success of the group and come to class prepared; they have read the articles and are ready to talk about them, perhaps recognizing that if they expect the other trainees to talk when they are facilitating, they must talk when others are in charge.

Finally, by structuring their groups' interactions, trainees are teaching; they are setting objectives, selecting important points, allocating time, and developing activities. Their facilitation of the groups is similar to microteaching situations.

Caveats and Options

1. At times, trainees are displeased with particular facilitators because they let the discussion ramble, talk too much themselves, allow other trainees to bring in too many personal anecdotes, or don't pinpoint the main concepts in the readings. The teacher educator may ask the groups to talk about these issues in their groups as they arise or provide more directed guidelines that might prevent some of these issues from developing in the first place.

Acknowledgment

I would like to thank Don McKay for allowing me to use his group plan in the narrative.

References and Further Reading

Richards, J. C., & Rodgers, T. (1987). Method, approach, design, and procedure. In M. H. Long & J. C. Richards (Eds.), *Methodology in TESOL: A book of readings* (pp. 145–157). Rowley, MA: Newbury House.

Stevick, E. W. (1980). *Teaching languages: A way and ways.* Rowley: MA: Newbury House.

Video: A Tool for Reflection

Contributor
Carol Houser Piñeiro
*Boston University,
United States*

Narrative

At the beginning of a particularly hectic fall semester during which I had to supervise 26 novice teachers*, I made a proposition to the group. If any were willing to participate in a project that would help them look more closely at their teaching, they would be excused from my customary class visits and evaluations. Five women and one man, all of whom were TESOL MEd candidates, volunteered. They ranged in experience from Gerry, who had only tutored ESL for a few months, to Hilary, who had taught French for many years.

At an orientation meeting, I passed out notebooks and told the novice teachers that they were to choose one of the two classes they had been assigned and, once a week, after teaching, to write about it. I did not tell them what or how to write, but simply to reflect on it in their journals for 15–20 minutes. I also told them that they would videotape that same class at the beginning, middle, and end of the semester, and watch the tapes. Besides their usual reflection after the class, they would make another journal entry after they had watched the tape. During the semester, I would meet with them and watch a segment of their choosing from each tape and listen to them talk about it. When a novice teacher remarked that one of her classes was easier to teach than the other, I commented that perhaps she should choose the more difficult one for the project. Although not quite sure of exactly what to expect, the novice teachers began writing in their journals and videotaping their classes.

I did not look at the journals during the semester because I had planned to study them in depth at the conclusion of the project. Rather, I met with each of the teachers three times and watched segments of their tapes. Situations that they found confusing or felt unable to deal with came up:

*Editor's note: We use the term *novice teacher* because the 26 trainees referred to here are graduate students in TESOL while teaching in Boston University's Intensive English Program.

120

student apathy toward class activities, talkative students not giving quieter ones a turn. They asked me to advise them on some of these problems, but instead of offering suggestions, I asked them to brainstorm a little and come up with ideas themselves, hoping that this process of reflection, coupled with the TESOL classes they were taking, would point them in the right direction.

At the end of the semester, I met with the group and asked them to summarize their experiences in their journals. In general, they felt that reflecting on their classes had been valuable because it enabled them to focus subjectively on certain areas of teaching and to record what was happening from week to week. Videotaping their classes allowed them to focus objectively on other areas from a different perspective. They all agreed that although it had been more time-consuming than simple class visits and evaluations, it was probably more effective because they were conscious of developing their own skills and strategies for understanding their teaching.

Procedure

1. Explain the project to the trainees and ask for volunteers. Note: This activity is most appropriate for trainees or teachers who are responsible for teaching their own classes.
2. At an orientation meeting, hand out notebooks and tell the trainees to choose a particular class they are teaching and to reflect on it in writing each week for 15–20 minutes.
3. Make up a schedule for the trainees' classes to be videotaped. Trainees make appointments with you to show their tapes and talk about them.
4. Trainees make journal entries about their classes every week and videotape them at the beginning, middle, and end of the semester. After they watch the tape, they make an extra journal entry reflecting on what they have seen.
5. Schedule meetings with each trainee to watch segments of the tapes. When asked for advice, help the trainee brainstorm for ideas instead of giving direct suggestions.
6. Have trainees make a final journal entry about their experiences and call a meeting at the end of the semester to get feedback on the project.

7. Trainees either keep their journals for future reference or return them to you for perusal.

Rationale

Because our program has more than 600 language students, and because I teach as well as perform administrative duties, it is almost impossible to give much personal attention to the novice teachers. Class visits and evaluations twice a semester plus weekly training sessions on different techniques are all I am able to provide. From the emphasis in current literature on developing teachers' abilities to reflect on their practice, it has occurred to me that journal writing and videotaping, because they are activities that novice teachers can engage in on their own, may serve as an effective means of personalizing their experience in our highly impersonal program. A novice like Gerry was able to identify an aspect of teaching that he felt needed improvement, such as getting the quieter students to participate in class discussions, and work on it all semester. Hilary was able to experiment with different techniques for teaching an advanced ESL class that she had never used while teaching French classes and evaluate their effectiveness. If there had been enough equipment to go around, I would have encouraged all the novice teachers to participate in these videotaping and journal writing activities.

Caveats and Options

1. Some novice teachers find it difficult to watch themselves on video-tape the first time around, and one even described it as "extremely painful." I try to assure them that the tapes are for their own viewing, reflection, and growth. This is why I watch only a segment of their choice rather than an entire class.
2. If the institution does not have access to video equipment, audiotape recorders can be used; instead of written journals, journals on audio-cassettes can also be kept.
3. Although there were only 6 novice teachers, I sometimes found it difficult to keep the viewing appointments because there were 20 other teachers to visit and evaluate twice a semester. To make matters easier, you can suggest that the novice teachers share journals and videotapes with each other or with a more experienced master teacher.

4. On the whole, I think this activity is valuable because it gives novice teachers the tools with which to look more closely at their own teaching and development over time, a practice that can continue throughout their careers.

References and Further Reading

Clift, R. T., Houston, W. R., & Pugach, M. C. (1990). *Encouraging reflective practice in education.* New York: Teachers College Press.

Fosnot, C. T. (1989). *Enquiring teachers, enquiring learners.* New York: Teachers College Press.

Schon, D. A. (1983). *Educating the reflective practitioner.* San Francisco: Jossey-Bass.

Two Lessons Within a Lesson: Strategies for Teaching Concepts, Rules, and Generalizations

Contributor
Willis E. Poole
Rhode Island College,
United States

Narrative

The teacher educator, Jerry, begins the class by telling the trainees that they are going to learn about two teaching strategies that they can use to teach concepts, rules, or generalizations in their respective content areas. Upon hearing this, the trainees sit back and prepare to take notes. Jerry surprises them by saying that he is not going to tell them what these strategies are. They must instead discover them on their own. He divides the trainees into two groups: Observers and students. The observers are told that they will view two demonstrations, each exemplifying a different teaching strategy. They are to record the steps for each strategy. The other trainees will participate in the demonstrations.

Demonstration 1

Jerry begins the first demonstration by telling the trainees that they are going to discover the characteristics of a new organism in biology, the name of which will be kept secret until they can define it. He shows the trainees one example of the organism, then asks them to tell him what they think the characteristics are that define it (see below).

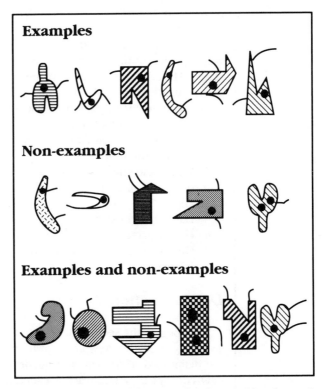

The trainees suggest that it has equal sides, a tail, a butterfly shape, a big eye, and is covered with stripes. Jerry writes these characteristics on the blackboard without comment, then reveals another example of the concept, asking, "Now what do you think the characteristics are that define it?" As the trainees speak, he refines the list of characteristics, and then shows third and fourth examples of the organism while asking the trainees to tell what the characteristics are. Finally, they all agree on a black spot, stripes, and two "tails."

Jerry then shows the trainees three more pictures and asks them to tell him whether these are examples. The trainees examine the pictures and indicate that they are not examples of the organism and explain why. The process continues with trainees identifying examples and non-examples of the concept.

When Jerry then asks the trainees to define the organism in their own words, they say that it's an organism with a black spot, stripes, and two "tails." He tells them they have just defined a *Markino,* and then gives them a handout and asks them to identify other examples of Markinos.

At this point, Jerry asks the observers to outline the steps he used to teach the concept of a Markino. These steps are written on the blackboard under the heading, *Teaching Strategy 1:*

1. Explain the task.
2. While showing examples and non-examples of the organism, ask questions to help trainees identify the critical attributes of the concept.
3. Have trainees define the concept.
4. Give a name to the concept trainees have defined.
5. Give new examples to provide further practice in identifying the concept.

Demonstration 2

Jerry begins the second demonstration by telling the trainees that they are going to learn a new concept in geometry, and he reviews with them the definitions of triangle and quadrilateral and then tells them that the new concept they will learn is called a *Grote,* which he defines as either a shaded quadrilateral or an unshaded triangle. The trainees are shown examples and are asked to say why they are Grotes; he then shows non-examples of the concept and they are asked to explain why. Next, he mixes examples and non-examples and asks them to identify the Grotes and to justify their choices. Finally, he gives them a handout with new examples of Grotes and non-Grotes and asks them to select the Grotes (see below).

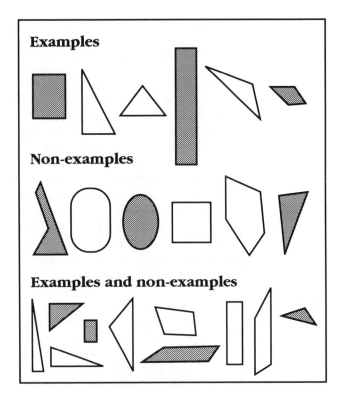

At this point, Jerry asks the observers to outline the steps he has used to teach the concept of a Grote. He writes these steps on the blackboard under the heading, *Teaching Strategy 2:*

1. Explain the task.
2. Assess prerequisite knowledge.
3. Name and define the concept.
4. Provide examples and non-examples of the concept, and have trainees identify the examples of the concept and say why they are examples of the concept and why others are not.
5. Give examples to provide further practice in identifying the concept.

Comparing the Demonstrations

Now Jerry asks the whole class to examine the steps used in each teaching strategy and to identify the essential characteristics that distinguish them. After discussion, they realize that in Teaching Strategy 1, the students discover the definition of the concept by examining examples and non-examples, and then the teacher names it. In Teaching Strategy 2, the teacher gives the definition and gives students practice in identifying examples of the concept. Jerry asks the trainees to define each teaching strategy in their own words while he writes the definitions on the blackboard. He then tells them they have defined an *inductive teaching strategy* (Teaching Strategy 1) and an *expository teaching strategy* (Teaching Strategy 2).

Jerry remains silent for a few moments and then asks the class "By the way, what strategy did I use today to teach you these two teaching strategies?" There is silence and then suddenly everyone starts talking at once, realizing that they have, in fact, experienced the Inductive Teaching Strategy for the whole class period.

Procedure

1. Tell trainees that today they will learn about two different teaching strategies that can be used to teach concepts, rules, or generalizations. They will observe two demonstrations and are to write the steps used in each strategy. At the end of the lesson, they will be asked to define each of the strategies in their own words.
2. Divide trainees randomly into two groups: The observers record the steps used in each strategy; the students take part in the two lessons.
3. Demonstrate the inductive teaching strategy:
   a. Introduce it by saying: "Today you are going to discover the characteristics of a new concept in biology. The name will be a secret until you all can define it. You will find the meaning of the concept by searching for the essential characteristics that define it."
   b. Provide hands-on experience with the concept: Ask questions to identify critical attributes, show examples, show non-examples, mix examples and non-examples.

    c. Have students define the concept in their own words and then name it after they have finished.

    d. Offer other examples to provide further practice.

4. Have the observers describe steps used in Teaching Strategy 1 while you write the steps on the board.

5. Demonstrate an expository teaching strategy.

    a. Introduce it by saying, "In previous classes you have learned the concepts triangle and quadrilateral. Today you are going to learn the meaning of a new concept in geometry. This new concept is called a Grote."

    b. Define the concept as "either a shaded quadrilateral or an unshaded triangle."

    c. Show examples and non-examples, first individually and then mixing them. Offer other examples to provide further practice.

6. Have the observers describe steps used in Teaching Strategy 2 while you write the steps on the board.

7. Have the trainees as a group define the teaching strategies by describing the differences and similarities between them, stating the critical attributes of each, and defining both teaching strategies.

8. Label the teaching strategies and check for understanding by asking which strategy was used to conduct the activity.

Rationale

The purpose of this activity is to introduce the trainees to two teaching strategies that they can use when they become teachers. The activity used to present the lesson is an inductive teaching strategy, thus providing trainees with hands-on experiences with both expository and inductive teaching strategies. Although the concepts used in each of the demonstration lessons are invented ones, they provide the experience of actually feeling what it is like to learn with these strategies. In addition, the trainees have a high level of interest and involvement in the lesson because they are discovering the steps used in teaching with these strategies.

Caveats and Options

1. This activity can be used with trainees in any content subjects. The only requirement is to select material that is new to the trainees you are teaching. For example, if none of your trainees has a knowledge

of Spanish, you could teach them the rule that nouns and adjectives have to agree in both number and gender.

2. You can also vary the procedure by having different observers for each demonstration lesson. If trainees are the observers for the first demonstration lesson, they could be the students in the second one.

3. If you want trainees to be observers only, you can videotape two minilessons exemplifying these strategies. You can then have trainees observe and analyze the similarities and differences between the two teaching strategies.

Handout 8

Markinos and Grotes

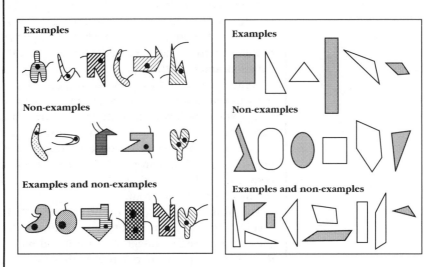

The design of these figures was suggested by drawings from the Elementary Science Study of Education Development Center, Inc., Newton, MA.

Poole, W.E. Two lessons within a lesson: Strategies for teaching concepts, rates, and generalizations. In D. Freeman, with Steve Cornwell (Eds.), *New ways in teacher education.* Alexandria, VA: TESOL.

Planning for Success

Contributor
John Raby
*Oxford University
Press, Taiwan*

Narrative

At a recent book-related teacher training workshop in Taiwan for Chinese teachers of English to adults, I started in a way that allowed me to introduce some overall methodological goals, find out what sort of previous teacher training teachers had received, find out something about their teaching situation, and have them perform a warm-up group activity of the sort that I would recommend they use with their own students. I also wanted to demonstrate a nonjudgmental approach as a teacher and show one way to get students involved in the administration of classroom activities. I asked the teachers to divide into groups of six and asked each group to introduce themselves and choose a group leader. I then modeled what to do with one group and asked the group leaders of the other groups to copy what I did. I distributed a handout with six different statements to the members of one group.

The group leaders copied the procedure in their groups. Group members received one statement that they read aloud in turn and then said whether she or he agreed or disagreed with it and why. Finally, the reader asked the other group members whether they agreed or disagreed.

Six Statements

1. I plan to use 100% English in my classes. Using Chinese, the native language, destroys the English-speaking environment that I'm trying to create.

2. I plan to speak as little as possible in class. I know that if I'm talking, I'm probably denying my students an English-speaking opportunity.

3. I plan to let my students personalize their learning. Just doing things that are in the book without letting them relate this to their lives is very forgettable.

4. I plan to include lots of review phases in my class: at the beginning, in the middle, at the end, after a few weeks. It's very easy to forget something if you don't review it.

5. I plan to elicit words and structures from my students rather than teach these. It's amazing but one student in the class usually already knows what I'm trying to teach.

6. I plan to use as much pair and group work as possible. I know that it relaxes my students and increases their speaking opportunities. It allows me to walk around and monitor their progress.

When this was finished, working with the group as a whole, I asked a volunteer to read each statement aloud and offer an opinion about it. Then I invited other contrary views from the rest of the group. The ensuing discussion took only a little moderating. I avoided making statements about my own views but did throw in a controversial opinion or two to stir up the debate. The one I remember best relates to the amount of translation one should use: "It depends," said one respondent. "Oh you mean, in a beginners' class you wouldn't translate but in an advanced class, it's OK?" I responded, purposefully reversing the usual assumptions about translation. My main task was to decide how quickly to move on to the next statement. At the end, I told the teachers that I felt that all six statements were goals that were worth working toward and that they could be used to assess one's progress as a teacher. This set the scene for the rest of the workshop, which was on lesson planning.

Procedure

1. Prepare enough copies of the statements for the number of participants. Cut up the individual statements, but keep them in complete sets.
2. Ask the participants to divide into groups of six. With five members, drop one statement; with seven, the group leader does not get a statement.
3. Group members introduce themselves to each other and appoint a group leader.
4. Select one group and ask group leaders from other groups to copy what you do with them. Ask individual group members to choose a number from 1 to 6, and distribute the statements by number. Ask each member to read aloud the statement, comment on it, and ask the other members if they agree or disagree. The group leader selects the order in which the statements are read and watches the time. Step out of this group and move around to monitor the progress of all groups.
5. After 6 minutes, or longer if necessary, call the groups back together and ask who has Statement 1. Invite one respondent to read it aloud and express agreement or disagreement. Invite other opinions from the rest of the class. Continue the process with Statement 2 and so on.

Rationale

I have found from experience that if you want to run an interactive workshop in which teachers participate fully, you need to set the stage. When I have given an overlong speech to introduce a workshop, the workshop has generally suffered because the teachers have been reticent for the rest of the time. I firmly believe in warm-up activities for all classes: Language students may need them to begin thinking in English, and language teachers may need to start thinking about methods and techniques. I also want to put out suggestions without imposing them in a top-down way. At the beginning of a workshop with teachers I have never met before, I need a quick way to find out how they are thinking and to establish a rapport with them. This activity can take 15–20 minutes, and the interaction generated makes it very worthwhile.

Caveats and Options

1. Putting the statements in simple language relating to classroom experience from the teacher's perspective is important.
2. Giving each individual teacher ownership of one statement is the magic touch that brings the activity alive.
3. Six statements (plus or minus one) seem just right for this activity.
4. The activity can be amended to use statements on topics (e.g., error correction, use of specific translation, the role of practice). It can also be structured to deal with fact—i.e., which statements are true or false—when the statements are drawn from a common reading or previous presentation.

Adapted Case Studies: A Problem-Solving Approach to Teacher Education

Contributor
Helen Raptis
McGill University,
Canada

The adapted case study activity can be used in teacher education programs to deal with the concept of discipline within the context of language classrooms.

Narrative

As part of a graduate program in teaching ESL, trainees are required to do a 2-month internship. As the teacher educator in charge of their internship, I observe them on a regular basis. Prior to the observation, the trainees turn in lesson plans. In addition to dealing with routine issues that come up in the practicum, I gather ethnographic data. In this case, I looked for examples of disruptive or undisciplined behavior. When I came across an example of undisciplined behavior, I used the data to design a case study. This adapted case study links the moments when behavior deteriorated to gaps or problems in the lesson plan.

In class, I use the case study to lead the trainees through four key phases. First, in groups of three, they read the lesson plan as well as the observations of the lesson execution. They are asked to isolate points in the lesson where unacceptable student behavior occurs. Second, the groups modify the lesson plan to prevent future undisciplined behavior. Third, the trainees report their solutions to their peers in a class discussion. As a follow-up, the trainees examine samples of very sparse lesson plans and predict where difficulties may arise in the lesson execution. They then amplify or rewrite the problematic lesson plans in an attempt to prevent such behavioral problems. Finally, trainees analyze their own plans to determine where they see gaps in the planning stage that could lead to undisciplined student behavior. They amplify their own plans with the goal of preventing such problems in their classrooms.

Procedure

1. Prior to the lesson, collect ethnographic classroom data by observing trainees while practice teaching.
2. Analyze, adapt, and copy a plan and observations of a class in which language students display disruptive, undisciplined behavior.
3. In class, review techniques for reacting to discipline problems. Introduce the idea that sometimes otherwise well-behaved students demonstrate undisciplined behavior in reaction to the classroom situation or activities. Distribute the case studies to trainees.
4. In groups of three or four, have trainees analyze the case studies (see Handout 9), list problems in the execution of the lesson, and solve them by looking for gaps in the lesson plan.
5. Ask the trainees to modify the lesson plans to take care of the gaps they have identified.
6. Have the groups report their findings and solutions in a whole class discussion.
7. Give the trainees a sparse lesson plan, telling them to find gaps, predict trouble spots in the lesson, and rewrite the plan based on their predictions.
8. Have trainees analyze their own lesson plans to avert potential off-task behavior.

Rationale

This adapted case study activity encourages a problem-solving approach to teacher education that can augment traditional lecture, demonstration, and discussion techniques. It is trainee centered and promotes a view of teaching as an ongoing process of planning, reflection, assessment, and adaptation. It also approximates the case study methodology that has been used successfully in law and business for over a century (Shulman, 1991).

Caveats and Options

1. The technique is best implemented in the latter part of the methodology course because trainees may not be able to solve the problems before the principles of teaching and learning have been dealt with.

2. The activity can be adapted in limitless ways because the data, which provide the focus of the case, are collected, modified, and presented in the context of their trainees' field experiences.
3. One option is to assign the adapted case study to trainees individually and have them submit their solutions either to the class or for assessment by the teacher educator.
4. When using the activity, the names, context, and original lesson should be altered in order to maintain the anonymity of the trainee and students whose classroom data are being used.
5. It is crucial to emphasize that there are no right or wrong answers to the problems presented. The object of the activity is to develop a problem-solving approach to teaching, in which self-assessment is vital. The power to analyze teaching behavior is important for professional growth.
6. It should also be stressed that teachers are not to blame for students' undisciplined behavior. Much undisciplined behavior originates outside of the classroom context. The preventive approach advocated here allows us to ensure that, due to insufficient planning, we do not contribute to undisciplined behavior.

References and Further Reading

Richards, J. C., & Nunan, D. (Eds.). (1990). *Second language teacher education*. New York: Cambridge University Press.

Shulman, J. H. (1991). Revealing the mysteries of teacher-written cases: Opening the black box. *Journal of Teacher Education, 42*(4), 250–262.

Handout 9

Adapted Case Study

Introduction

Disciplinary difficulties can be divided into two types: those to which we can only react and those that we can try to prevent. Problems to which we can only react often originate from situations outside of the classroom. Reaction to and treatment of such problems must reflect the philosophy of the teacher, the administration, and the community at large. On the other hand, preventing disruptive student behavior requires focused preteaching preparation. In lesson preparation, teachers must ask themselves fundamental questions such as What do I want my students to do? Why? How? We need to analyze our plan and anticipate where problems might arise in lesson execution. Look at the following plans as well as the observations of the class.

Task

Underline trouble spots in the lesson execution and decide what modifications you would make to the plan to avoid such difficulties in the classroom.

Raptis, H. (1993). Adapted case studies: A problem-solving approach to teacher education. In D. Freeman, with S. Cornwell (Eds.), *New ways in teacher education*. Alexandria, VA: TESOL.

A. Plan

Objectives: Students (Ss) will identify clothing when questioned
Target group: Grade 4; Francophone learners of English

Presentation: Teacher (T) uses realia to elicit clothing from Ss; T names if Ss can't; Ss name or listen while T presents clothing (10 min)

Manipulation: Ss fill in names of clothing with teacher (on handout) (10 min)

Communication: In groups of six, Ss ask each other in groups what their favorite clothes are (15 min); Ss report back on what they've found out (5 min)

Follow-up, if time: Have Ss color the clothing with crayons for next lesson

B. Execution

8:30 T elicits or presents clothing using "real" clothes; Ss listen (many Ss not listening and chatting to each other)

8:35 T hands out worksheet with pictures of clothing; Ss fill in clothing with teacher's instructions; Example of T's language: "What's this? Shirt, good. S-H-I-R-T"; Ss who aren't good listeners get lost; give up and don't fill in clothing vocabulary; these trainees begin chatting, writing notes; T reprimands them

8:37 Two student trainees hand out grid for group work

8:40 T tells Ss to put themselves into groups of 6; Ss start grabbing friends, running across the room, shouting, etc.; T reprimands Ss for shouting, being unruly

8:44 T tells Ss that they will need pencils; Ss go back to desks, get pencils etc.

8:45 T instructs Ss to (a) choose a group leader, (b) start with leader, ask each other what favorite clothes are; Ss confused, ask what to do; T runs from group to group explaining in L1; By the time T explains to last group, Group 1 is finished and chatting in French; teacher reprimands them; Ss have not written each others' responses; T reprimands them

8:55 T asks groups to report on each other; Ss fidgeting and restless; two at back begin to throw erasers; T reprimands them

9:00 T asks Ss to return to desks

Raptis, H. (1993). Adapted case studies: A problem-solving approach to teacher education. In D. Freeman, with S. Cornwell (Eds.), *New ways in teacher education.* Alexandria, VA: TESOL.

9:03 T tells Ss to use crayons to color clothing as they wish; T tells Ss that worksheet will be used for activity next day
9:10 Bell rings

Sample of Sparse Lesson Plan

A. *Plan*

Objectives: Ss will be able to understand the sportscast on television
Target group: Grade 5; mixed language and cultural backgrounds; learning English
Activity 1: T puts Ss in groups of three to play Bingo (2 min)
Bingo games in groups of three to review numbers (13 min)
T circulates and helps students as needs arise
Activity 2: T reminds students of sports vocabulary from previous day (2 min)
T plays video of sportscasts (6 min)
T checks comprehension (3 min)
Follow-up: Review sports vocabulary on board (4 min)
Ss do sports worksheet individually (10 min)

Raptis, H. (1993). Adapted case studies: A problem-solving approach to teacher education. In D. Freeman, with S. Cornwell (Eds.), *New ways in teacher education.* Alexandria, VA: TESOL.

Teachers and Teacher Educators Learning Through Dialogue Journals

Contributors
Nancy Rhodes and
Donna Christian
*Center for Applied
Linguistics, United
States*

Narrative

Dialogue journals are written conversations, usually between a teacher and an individual student, that take place regularly and continually throughout an entire semester or school year (Peyton & Reed, 1990). In dialogue journal writing in an ESL classroom, students write regularly in a journal and the teacher responds, without evaluating or correcting the writing, as a partner in a conversation. The value of the dialogue journal lies in the open exchange of ideas that can occur and the concerned and warm acceptance by the teacher of the student's writing.

This program had three components: (a) a summer institute in which teachers received training in specific techniques for integrating language and content instruction and materials on which integrated lessons could be based; (b) school-based meetings, dialogue journals, and classroom observations during the following school year through which teacher educators supported the teachers in putting knowledge from (a) into practice; and (c) fall and spring meetings of the teachers to allow for further sharing of experiences, materials, and ideas across school sites.

We set out to see whether we could achieve these benefits using dialogue journals between teachers and teacher educators who were involved in a training project that focused on the integration of language and content instruction. We wanted to encourage communication between elementary school teachers, both ESL and classroom, and teacher educators, to help them, through their writing, to reflect on what they had learned in the project's training institute and monitor their teaching activities as they implemented new techniques. Throughout the school year, the teachers used the dialogue journal writing for a variety of purposes, including commenting on implementation of methods and techniques, asking for suggestions or advice about their teaching, clarifying ideas, reflecting on themselves as teachers, and expressing opinions about the training project.

The following are some of the exchanges between an ESL teacher and one of the teacher educators. In the first entry, the teacher writes about implementing ideas about a science-based ESL lesson she learned at the project's training institute. She also asks for suggestions on how to improve her students' journal writing. The teacher educator responds by giving suggestions for student journal writing and asking if the teacher followed through with the idea for a debate that she had mentioned in her first entry.

Teacher entry   November 1991

[The other ESL teacher] and I have been reinforcing the science curriculum of the sixth graders during some of our ESL time. Right now they're on astronomy and the kids are <u>so</u> excited about it. It's really neat to see! They're fascinated by stars, planets, moons, etc. Of course we're getting some big debate on the question of whether there is life on other planets. Hey, writing that just brought to mind an idea: Why not have a debate on that topic and have the kids be on 2 teams, research their side, and organize and present their arguments? I might do it!

I've also started the kids on their journals. Some students are very excited about it and want to keep writing and writing. Others do <u>not</u> want to write anything. I'm lucky if I can get a couple sentences from them. Any ideas on how to motivate these types?

Teacher educator response   December 1991

With regard to the journal writing with unwilling kids, I think it's fine if they just write a sentence or two (at least they write something!). Sometimes it takes months for students to build up confidence to write more, or to realize that they can really communicate with someone that way. Are <u>you</u> doing dialogue journals or just personal journals? The most important thing is that they generate the ideas and thoughts and can write about topics that interest them. I'll be curious to hear how they do as the year goes on.

P.S. Did you do the planet debate?

In the next response, the teacher comments on the meeting of project participants, describes an activity that she learned at the meeting, talks about how she adapted a suggestion from the teacher educator, and follows up on her earlier introduced topic of a class debate about life on other planets.

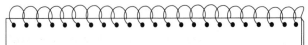

Teacher response   January 1992

[Our school] enjoyed the reunion in December. It was very practical, down-to-earth, and encouraging. What's more, I felt like a professional which is sometimes hard to feel in a school system....
[A classroom teacher] and I used the map-making idea from [the school that presented the idea at the reunion meeting] to team teach a map puzzle of South America. The kids loved it and it turned out to be neat!

In your letter your told me about the idea you used for Thanksgiving. I used the same thing for winter vocabulary and it really worked. You're right— it is more student-generated, which is an area I neet to work on. Thanks for the idea!

Yes, we did end up doing the debate, but in a modified form. We wrote things on the board that the students said about the topic: life on other planets. Then they used books to support or refute their statements, first on paper, then orally. It worked, but I'd like to try a real debate at some point.

In regard to the dialogue journals my class is doing: That was a good point about how it takes time to build up confidence to write. With one of the students that was reluctant to write, I think we've finally found a subject that he's interested in and it seems to help. He also loves to ask me questions, which I answer and then ask him questions.

The writing helped the teacher to reflect on her teaching and clarify her ideas by thinking on paper; it also gave the teacher educator a chance to hear the teacher's reactions to the training workshops and to see which techniques and strategies the teacher was able to implement in her classroom. A lot of information emerged through the written dialogue that would not have otherwise, information that helped the teacher educator to refine the training program and to adjust the activities for the next session.

Procedure

1. Introduce the idea of dialogue journals to trainees and/or teachers stressing that it is "a conversation between a teacher and an individual student. It is written, it is completely private; and it takes place regularly and continually throughout an entire school year or semester...." (Peyton & Reed, 1990, p. 3). Outline the purpose of keeping a journal: to increase opportunities for communication between you and trainees/teachers, and to allow for them to reflect on their experiences and get your direct feedback. In this way, you can individualize their learning.
2. Discuss procedural issues:
   a. How participants will keep the journal: notebook, computer, etc.
   b. How often they will write and how often you will respond, and whether it is an optional or required activity.
3. As the trainees/teachers begin to write, define any topics you want them to focus on. Encourage them to write regularly, as much as they want, and about topics of their own choice. The process of journal writing continues the length of the course or training session.
4. At the end of the course, evaluate the journal process, asking participants in their journals to evaluate its benefits and problems. Then, as a group, have the trainees/teachers discuss the pros and cons of interactive writing.

Rationale

We selected dialogue journal writing as one optional aspect of our teacher education project because it was felt that it would be an additional way for teachers to continue to evaluate, revise, and question what they had learned at the summer institute and to decide how they could adapt the techniques for their teaching. We hoped that it would also give us a good sense of what they had learned from the training, where we could improve, and how we could contribute to their learning in other ways not already anticipated.

Caveats and Options

1. In our training project, we did not require the dialogue journal writing and few teachers decided to participate. They may have been uneasy about the idea of starting a journal or just extremely busy with teaching, and understandably so. However, because we found it to be such a successful way of continuing interaction and enhancing communication with the teachers, in the future we will require it.
2. To lessen the time burden, we will suggest that participants keep journals for a semester instead of for an academic year.
3. As a variation, teachers can write dialogue journals with each other. Such cojournaling can work effectively to clarify ideas; however, it does not offer the personalized expert input that teacher educator-teacher pairs do.

References and Further Reading

Brinton, D., & Holten, C. (1989). What novice teachers focus on: The practicum in TESL. *TESOL Quarterly, 23,* 343–350.

Peyton, J. K., & Reed, L. (1990). *Dialogue journal writing with nonnative English speakers: A handbook for teachers.* Alexandria, VA: TESOL.

Roderick, J. (1986). Dialogue writing: Context for reflecting on self as teacher and researcher. *Journal of Curriculum and Supervision, 1,* 305–315.

Roderick, J., & Berman, L. (1984). Dialoguing about dialogue journals: Teachers as learners. *Language Arts, 61,* 686–692.

Peer Observation

Contributors
Jack C. Richards and
Charles Lockhart
*City Polytechnic of
Hong Kong, Hong Kong*

Narrative

Cedrick and Algernon are colleagues in a private language school. They are both teaching upper-intermediate conversation classes of young adult students. The course meets twice a week for 10 weeks. The two teachers have decided to observe each other's classes during the term and have scheduled two visits each. Before each visit, they usually meet for 10 minutes to discuss the observation. If Algernon is going to observe, Cedrick briefly runs through his lesson plan and gives Algernon an observation task. This will reflect some aspect of his teaching that Cedrick is interested in having monitored more closely. For example, today Cedrick has asked Algernon to observe his *action zone,* that is, to note which particular students he interacts with during the lesson and how often. In order to make Algernon's observation task easier to accomplish, Cedrick has provided him with a seating plan for the class. Algernon will place a mark against each student's position on the seating plan each time Cedrick asks a question. Algernon will code differently teacher-to-student, student-to-teacher, and student-to-student interactions.

Algernon now seats himself at the back of the class and watches the lesson, coding the classroom interaction. At the end of the lesson, he gives Cedrick the information he has gathered. Later that day over coffee, they meet to discuss the observation. Cedrick is curious to discover that he had no interaction with more than a third of the students in the class during the lesson. He and Algernon discuss possible reasons for this and how this pattern of teacher-student interaction could be changed.

The following week, it is Algernon's turn to teach and Cedrick's turn to observe. This time Algernon asks Cedrick to observe two particular students in the class and to note anything he can on their participation in

147

the lesson, particularly the extent to which they seem to be engaged in the lesson. Algernon is concerned that these two students are having difficulties with the course and wants to monitor their performance more closely. Later they meet to discuss Cedrick's observation.

Procedure

1. Before beginning the observations, the two teachers meet to discuss the nature of the class observed, the kind of material being taught, the teacher's approach to teaching, the kinds of students in the class, typical patterns of interaction, and class participation, etc.
2. The teachers identify a focus for the observation. Some examples might include:
   - Organization of the lesson—the entry, structuring, and closure of the lesson.
   - Teacher's time management—allotment of time to different activities during the lesson.
   - Students' performance on tasks—the strategies, procedures, and interaction patterns employed by students in completing a task.
   - Time-on-task—the extent to which students were actively engaged during a task.
   - Teacher's questions and students' responses—the types of questions teachers asked during a lesson and the way students responded.
   - Students' performance during pair work—the way students completed a pair work task, the responses they made during the task, and the type of language they used.
   - Classroom interaction—teacher-student and student-student interaction patterns during a lesson.
   - Group work—students' use of L1 versus L2 during group work, students' time-on-task during group work, and the dynamics of group activities.
3. The teachers develop procedures for the observer to use. For example:
   - Timed samples—the observer notes down specific behavior displayed at specified time intervals during the lesson.

- Coding forms—the observer checks the appropriate category on a set of coded categories of classroom behaviors whenever a behavior is displayed during the lesson.
- Descriptive narrative (broad)—the observer writes a narrative summarizing the main events that occur during the lesson.
- Descriptive narrative (narrow)—the observer writes a narrative focusing on a particular aspect of a lesson. For example, the observer describes what a single student did and said throughout the lesson.

4. The observer visits his or her partner's class and completes the observation, using the procedure that both parties have agreed on.
5. The two teachers meet as soon as possible after the lesson. The observer reports on the information collected during the lesson and discusses it with the teacher.

Rationale

Peer observation can play an important part in a language teaching program because it develops collegiality, it enables teachers to observe different styles of teaching, and it provides opportunities for critical reflection on one's own teaching.

The value of observation increases if the observer knows what to look for. An observation that concludes with a comment such as "Oh, that was a really nice lesson" is not particularly helpful to either party. On the other hand, giving the observer a task, such as collecting information on student participation patterns during a lesson, provides a focus for the observer and collects useful information for the teacher.

Caveats and Options

1. Clear lines of communication about the nature and purpose of peer observation are essential from the very start. If viewed simply as another initiative from the administration, peer observation may be resisted.
2. To support peer observation, administrators can either offer to replace, or find a replacement for, the observing teacher to provide time to visit a colleague. This can underscore the administration's commitment to collegial development.
3. Teachers may initially react to peer observation as an assessment exercise and see little to gain personally from it. Peer observation

should be approached as an opportunity for teachers to help each other collect useful information that they cannot obtain on their own.

4. It is crucial to discuss the observation while it is still fresh, as soon as possible afterwards.

References and Further Reading

Richards, J., & Lockhart, C. (1992). Teacher development through peer observation. *TESOL Journal, 1,* 7–11.

A Trainee-Determined Syllabus in a Teacher Education Course

Contributor
Heidi Riggenbach
*University of
Washington, United
States*

Narrative

In an MA program in TESL, trainees in a pedagogical grammar course are assigned Celce-Murcia and Larsen-Freeman's (1983) *The Grammar Book*. On the first day of class, they are given descriptions of possible activities and assignments, framed with the teacher educator's opinions on her preferred minimal requirements. The trainees conduct the remainder of this class; their goal is to present to the teacher educator, on their second class meeting, a syllabus outlining the number and type of assignments they will be required to do, the weighting of each assignment in determining final course grade, and other in-class activities. Their syllabus, a collaborative effort, will not be finalized until it has been approved by the teacher educator.

Once the syllabus is fixed, the course proceeds until midterm, when the teacher educator and trainees discuss the course's effectiveness and make any necessary adjustments. Questions considered include: (a) Are trainees' stated needs being met? (b) Is the teacher educator satisfied with trainee learning and performance? At the end of the course, the teacher educator solicits feedback from the trainees as to the overall effectiveness of the course.

Procedure

1. Before meeting the class, plan the "ideal" course: topics to be covered, the essential readings, course requirements, assignments, and activities. At this time, assess the trainees and determine what you feel they will need of that content.
2. At the first class meeting, verify your assessment. The following questions may help: Is there high trainee awareness of their own course needs? Should they be allowed a great deal of autonomy? Do trainees

require structure and guidance? Should they be allowed less autonomy?

3. Present your syllabus preferences and options.
4. Have the trainees negotiate the syllabus, with or without you, depending on the amount of guidance needed.
5. At the second class meeting, ask the trainees to present their negotiated syllabus, which you approve or further negotiate.
6. Schedule a midterm assessment of the course to determine its effectiveness and address whether trainees' stated needs are being met and whether you are satisfied with their learning and performance.
7. Conduct a final assessment of the course at the end of the term.

Rationale

The recent trend of learner-centered approaches to language teaching has most often been applied to language learning situations and less so to teacher education programs. In programs with a practical orientation, trainee involvement in syllabus design is one method of learning by doing. Allowing trainees responsibility for determining their course of learning is a means of showing respect for their maturity and decision-making abilities. With this process, they must take responsibility for the decisions they make.

Caveats and Options

1. Trainee input into syllabus design will not work in all cases. Some trainees may be shy in expressing their opinions and preferences or they may not have good negotiating skills, so more verbal or domineering trainees may have more say in what is negotiated.
2. An imbalance in trainee ability level is a related problem. Some trainees may be highly motivated, well aware of their own needs and abilities, and capable of working both in groups and independently; others may not exhibit these qualities. If you are aware of such issues beforehand, you can participate as discussion leader in the syllabus design negotiations, drawing out the quieter trainees.
3. You can follow up the negotiations with written surveys on trainees' satisfaction with the negotiated syllabus and on their confidence in their peers' abilities to pull their own weight. Survey results may indicate whether intervention is necessary and changes may need to be made.

4. Trainees may simply resent doing all the work. They may, unfortunately, perceive the syllabus negotiation process as evidence of your laziness or lack of competence. For this reason, you need to take seriously the step of creating an initial syllabus (see Step 1 under Procedure), and of building in options for lectures, summaries, quizzes, and other more traditional teacher-centered approaches. There is no reason why such activities should not be part of the trainee-negotiated syllabus, if they represent a preferred method of learning.
5. The amount of decision making allowed trainees depends on your confidence in their maturity and their awareness of their needs in a particular course. It also reflects your comfort with loss of control in being the sole decision maker.

References and Further Reading

Celce-Murcia, M., & Larsen-Freeman, D. (1983). *The grammar book.* Rowley, MA: Newbury House.

Focused Observations Using Guide Questions

Contributor
Melinda Roth Sayavedra
Oregon State University, United States

Narrative

Three trainees, Yukiko, Naif, and Susan, prepare to observe a language class as part of their methods course. They will observe the class four times over the course of 15 weeks. The trainees each have a different set of questions to focus on during each observation. As they wait for the class to begin, they observe the students entering. The class has 12 students: 3 Koreans, 2 Japanese, 4 Mexicans, 2 Russians, and 1 Egyptian.

As the class gets underway, the trainees observe quietly, making notes as they notice an activity or action that addresses their questions. After the class, they thank the teacher and hurry off to their next class. Later that week, in their methodology class, they share with the teacher educator and other classmates what they saw.

Yukiko notes that she thought there were four activities but that it was hard to tell if the vocabulary activity on body parts was one activity or two, as it didn't ever come to closure (see Questions 2, 3, and 4 on Handout 10). Naif says he noticed that although the teacher never attempted to limit the use of the student's native languages in class, there wasn't much of it used. He also noted that when the teacher put students in groups, they were more animated and the classroom usually got louder (see Questions 15 and 20 on Handout 10).

After each trainees comments, the teacher educator leads a discussion on what they observed, what was effective, and what was less effective and how they might handle particular aspects of presenting a lesson or managing a classroom. The teacher educator asks what the observations tell the trainees about their own teaching. At the end of the class, the teacher educator assigns the questions for the next week's observations.

Procedure

1. Hand out the list of "Focused Observation Questions" (see Handout 10).
2. Select one to three questions from the list and ask trainees to focus on answering these during their observations.
3. Have the trainees observe ESL classes.
4. Meet with the trainees to discuss their focused observations.
5. Repeat Steps 2–4, focusing on different questions.

Rationale

In many training situations, trainees observe classes either as a part of a methods course or as a separate activity. Often, though, they are not sure exactly what they are supposed to be looking for when observing these classes. Using focused observation questions can make observations more meaningful, get trainees to think about how to present a lesson, or prevent or solve classroom management problems. The questions provide a starting point for discussion of these issues.

Caveats and Options

1. The questions listed can be adjusted. You can decide which questions will be most beneficial to the particular group or individual trainees at any given time.
2. Recommend that the trainees do some general observations to get an overall feel for a language class, especially at the beginning of their training period, and that a focused observation not be required each time.
3. Trainees can treat the list of questions as a menu from which they can select those most interesting to them.
4. Different individuals or groups can observe for different questions to provide a complete picture of the class.
5. The questions, either in part or in toto, can be used as an interview guide when talking with the teacher.

References and Further Reading

Fanselow, J. (1987). *Breaking rules: Generating and exploring alternatives in language teaching*. White Plains, NY: Longman.

Handout 10

Focused Observation Questions

1. How does the teacher focus the students' attention on the lesson at the beginning of class?
2. How many activities take place during one class period? What type of activities are they? In what order are they introduced? How much time is spent on each? Why?
3. How does the teacher move the class from one activity to another?
4. How does the teacher provide closure to an activity?
5. What learning objectives has the teacher set? How does the teacher let students know the objectives or learning outcomes of the lesson, activity, or unit?
6. Does the teacher stay focused on the lesson?
7. How does the teacher introduce new material?
8. How does the teacher check whether students understand what they are supposed to do during an activity?
9. What kind of guided practice does the teacher provide for the students?
10. What kind of independent practice does the teacher provide for the students?
11. When and how does the teacher review material?
12. Does the teacher use realia in the classroom? If so, in what ways?
13. How does the teacher end class?
14. When and how does the teacher take care of administrative duties such as taking attendance or handing back homework?
15. Are students actively participating in the lesson? Do they seem interested? Bored? Happy? Afraid? What makes you think so?
16. How does the teacher get students to participate?

Sayavedra, M. R. (1993). Focused observations using guide questions. In D. Freeman, with S. Cornwell (Eds.), *New ways in teacher education*. Alexandria, VA: TESOL.

17. How does the teacher get quiet students to participate more actively?
18. How does the teacher get students to speak loudly enough?
19. How does the teacher deal with students who are not paying attention?
20. Does the teacher attempt to limit the first languages spoken in the classroom? How?
21. How does the teacher make the material meaningful and relevant to these particular students?
22. How does the teacher give directions for an activity? Verbally? Visually? Through examples?
23. How does the teacher emphasize main points? Is there a change in the volume of the teacher's voice or in the rate of speech or in body language?
24. When and how does the teacher correct students' errors?
25. When and how does the teacher give encouragement or praise?
26. At what points during the lesson does the teacher write on the board or overhead? Why?
27. How many times does the teacher repeat a question or phrase? Does the teacher repeat the question or phrase verbatim or does the teacher paraphrase?
28. Are there certain times when the teacher seems to use repetition and others when the teacher paraphrases? Why is this?
29. Where is the teacher standing while giving instructions to the whole class? While eliciting answers from individuals in the class? While students are engaged in small-group or paired activities?
30. How does the teacher assign homework?
31. Do you notice any differences in how teachers deal with these issues with different class levels?

Sayavedra, M. R. (1993). Focused observations using guide questions. In D. Freeman, with S. Cornwell (Eds.), *New ways in teacher education.* Alexandria, VA: TESOL.

Course Versus Workshop: A Compromise

Contributor
Linda Schinke-Llano
Millikin University,
United States

Narrative

The following framework for in-service teacher education represents a compromise between the traditional semester- or quarter-length course at the one extreme and the one-topic, one-date workshop at the other. The approach presented here involves a teacher educator or a team of teacher educators, working at regular intervals throughout an academic year, with the ESL/EFL teachers of a school, district, or geographic region. A typical schedule might look like this:

Month	Days	Contact Hours
September	Thursday evening All day Friday All day Saturday	3 6 6
November	Friday evening All day Saturday	3 6
February	Friday evening All day Saturday	3 6
April	All day Friday All day Saturday	6 6
Total contact hours		45

The frequency, duration, format, and content of the visits are variable. As a result, the framework provides advantages to in-service teacher education that are lacking in both courses and workshops.

Procedure

1. Meet with teachers' representatives to determine the content. Use teachers' requests and/or observations of their teaching, as well as your areas of expertise and knowledge of the needs of similar groups of teachers to define the content.
2. Base the schedule on the teachers' needs, the financial resources of the administrative body, and the in-service time available. Your availability is also a factor.
3. Arrange the actual project so that it consists of on-site, between-session, and follow-up activities. On-site activities can include formal presentations, small-group work, classroom visits, and individual meetings with teachers regarding projects and goals. Between-session activities can include communication between teachers and teacher educators, small-group meetings of teachers, and readings. Follow-up activities can include self-evaluations by teachers and teacher educators, evaluations by teachers of teacher educators, and evaluations by teacher educators of teachers' projects and goals.

Rationale

Traditional approaches to in-service teacher education offered in courses and workshops have advantages and disadvantages. Courses can provide the in-depth analyses of subjects; however, they are rarely tailor-made for teachers from the same school, district, or geographic region. Workshops can afford access to visiting professionals, but can leave participants frustrated by a lack of applicability and continuity.

This framework offers the advantages of both courses and workshops and avoids their disadvantages. Although the focus is on teachers, teacher educators benefit from this framework as well. In traditional courses, the instructors usually do not see their students, the teachers, in classrooms. In workshops, the teacher educators leave not knowing whether the information provided is relevant and easily applicable. This approach avoids both of these drawbacks.

Caveats and Options

1. There is great flexibility in this framework. For example, the number of teacher educators can vary from an individual to teams of people, and the number of visits during an academic year can range from two to six or more, depending upon needs and resources. The duration of the visits is also flexible.
2. The format of the visits can include a combination of formal presentations, small-group work, classroom visits, and individual meetings with teachers to discuss year-long goals and projects.
3. The content can focus on a single issue, such as methodology, or can include multiple topics such as second language acquisition theory, methodology, or assessment.
4. If desired, district in-service credit or even university credit may be given.
5. Planning between teachers' representatives and teacher educators is crucial. The choice of representatives can be based on school, district, or region.

Multiple Evaluations of Oral Microteaching Assignments

Contributor
Dorothy Solé
University of Cincinnati, United States

Narrative

At a large public university, a three-credit graduate course has been developed to train international teaching assistants. On a given day, 6–12 prospective international teaching assistants can be observed asking general questions about the U.S. college system, commenting on and evaluating each other's written assignments, leading class discussions based on readings in the textbook, or giving previously prepared but ungraded minilessons based on teaching techniques that have been explained and modeled by the instructor. Self-and group critiquing follows to analyze the strengths and weaknesses of the discussion leader and the minilesson.

Three trainees have prepared longer, formally graded presentations, which are required in lieu of typical tests. Depending on the day, you might sit in on a brief introduction to an undergraduate course with a brief description of the syllabus, overview of the course, course requirements and grading procedure, or an explanation of a concept basic to the course. The "teacher" is using visual aids, examples and non-examples, and questions to clarify and check understanding. Or you might hear a 15-minute lecture about the historical development of a major theory in the field. The lecture is enhanced with visual aids, and time must be scheduled for questions from the audience.

These formal sessions are videotaped. Every member of the class evaluates the presentations on a short form prepared by the instructor, while the instructor takes notes for a holistic evaluation of the presentation. After the presentation, the speakers must view their own performance and produce a one- to one-and-a-half-page, typewritten self-evaluation answering the following questions:

1. What did I do well?

161

2. Where could I have improved?
3. How could this improvement be implemented?
4. What did I learn from this assignment?

The self-evaluations are exchanged for peer commentary and then turned in for feedback from the instructor. Finally, the entire packet of commentaries and evaluations is passed back to the student teacher.

Procedure

1. Prepare an oral presentation assignment, listing all major requirements and time limits.
2. Schedule videotaping equipment.
3. Give a short evaluation form to other trainees to fill out after each presentation. Each listener should have an evaluation packet with forms for each presentation the trainee will hear (see Handout 11).
4. Prepare your own evaluation forms.
5. On the day of the presentations, give each member of the class an evaluation packet and explain the peer evaluation assignment. Have the student teachers give their presentations. Fill out your evaluation sheet as the presentations are being done. Assign a self-evaluation paper.
6. On the day the self-evaluations are due, ask the trainees to exchange and comment on each other's papers with a short peer evaluation form. Comment on the self-evaluation yourself.
7. Return the entire packet, consisting of the teacher evaluation, peer evaluations, and self-evaluation, to the original presenter.

Rationale

There are several reasons for the basic design of the activity. Because the entire class is involved in the evaluation procedure, the presenter prepares for an audience. The presenter gets feedback from several sources—including you and peers. Because the objective of this course is to train graduate teaching assistants, who are often asked to grade or evaluate assignments, the participants get some experience in U.S. evaluation techniques. The self-evaluation assignment encourages trainees to watch themselves and analyze their successes and failures, think about reasons, and consider ways to self-correct the deficiencies.

Options and Caveats

1. Although most students gracefully accept the task of peer evaluation, some have voiced discomfort about it. Some do not like to criticize each other; others object to the "positive" orientation of the evaluations and do not like to have to find something good if the work is generally of poor quality. It is up to you to create a nonthreatening atmosphere where such communal critiquing is encouraged.
2. Because the course is graded only on a pass/fail basis, evaluations are limited to ratings of unacceptable, acceptable, or excellent.
3. The term *instructor* on the evaluation forms refers to the trainee who is making the minipresentation.

Handout 11

Sample Form for Peer Evaluation of Oral Presentation

Please listen to your classmate's presentation. Then answer the following questions:

What was the instructor's name? _____

What subject was s/he going to teach? _____

	Yes	No
Did you understand the main objectives of the course?	_____	_____
Were the requirements clearly stated?	_____	_____
Did you understand the grading system?	_____	_____
Did the instructor seem helpful?	_____	_____
Did the instructor look at the class?	_____	_____

Other comments:

Please rate this presentation:

   unacceptable _____   acceptable _____   excellent _____

This form was developed by Susan Jenkins, University of Cincinnati.

Solé, D. (1993). Multiple evaluations of oral microteaching assignments. In D. Freeman, with S. Cornwell (Eds.), *New ways in teacher education.* Alexandria, VA: TESOL.

Sample Form for Peer Evaluations of Written Self-Evaluations

Name of evaluator: _____

Name of author: _____

What was best about this self-evaluation?

How could this paper have been improved?

Please rate this self-evaluation:

unacceptable _____   acceptable _____   excellent _____

Solé, D. (1993). Multiple evaluations of oral microteaching assignments. In D. Freeman, with S. Cornwell (Eds.), *New ways in teacher education.* Alexandria, VA: TESOL.

Reflection on Being a Student in a Foreign Language Classroom

Contributor
Amy L. Tickle
Michigan State University, United States

Narrative

This activity is designed to help trainees analyze what students learn from communicative activities and to reflect on being a student in a foreign/second language classroom.

A class of trainees is divided into five groups of four. Each person is given a sentence from a strip story. The material for the strip story describes common objects in very scientific or technical terms. Each group has a different description. For example, John's strip reads:

> HMWA is a sedentary-mode ergonomic workstation with the capacity to support gravitational hard-copy file manager, planar processing field, and a random access information manifold.

In the same group, Bob receives a strip that reads:

> It is used with a task-motivating somatic positioner with contoured ischial platform.

John's group works hard trying to reconstruct the original paragraph. The group moans, however, when the teacher educator tells them that they are not allowed to show their papers to each other. After about 30 minutes, the group thinks they have their paragraph in the correct order.

John asks the teacher educator to come over and check. Their paragraph reads:

Hard-Copy Multitask Window Array

HMWA is a sedentary-mode ergonomic workstation with the capacity to support gravitational hard-copy file manager, planar processing field, and a random access information manifold. The HMWA is used for inter-ruptive sequential bio-optical scanning, psychomotor-actuated text generation and arithmetic operations, featuring visually discriminable nonvolatile off-line storage with prehensile data retrieval, and operator-resident processing protocols for alphanumeric graphic input and outputs. It is used with a task-motivating somatic positioner with contoured ischial platform.

After all groups finish ordering their paragraphs, the trainees are asked to first reflect on what students can learn from this activity. They mention parts of speech, word forms, cohesion devices, and then talk about what they have learned as trainees. The activity has heightened their awareness of having a sound rationale for communicative activities. Because the language is difficult, the trainees also empathize with how students feel during activities, and they better understand the strategies used to accomplish the task. They also critique certain aspects of the activity from a student's point of view. The trainees are encouraged to consider these points when planning future lessons.

Procedure

1. Before class, cut the paragraphs into sentences.
2. In class, put the names of the objects on the board.
3. Put the trainees into groups and give each person a piece of paper with one sentence/clause on it. Each group collectively has the description of one object.
4. Ask the trainees to put the strips in the proper order. They are to read their sentences without showing them to other members of the group.
5. When the trainees have the paragraphs in order, ask one person from each group to read the paragraph. Then, in open discussion, see if the other groups agree with the arrangement. Encourage discussion of the strategies trainees have used for combining sentences. If necessary, identify the groups whose paragraphs are still not correct and encourage more discussion until the paragraph is correct.
6. Give the trainees the complete, reconstructed paragraphs and ask them to guess what the object is. Have them identify the clues and strategies that were used in ordering each paragraph.

7. Ask the trainees to reflect in writing on the following questions: (a) What will students learn from this activity? (b) What did you as trainees learn from this activity? Ask them to discuss their answers.

Rationale

As a teacher educator, my experience has been that trainees are able to use communicative activities in the classroom, but they are often unable to articulate to themselves or the students the rationales for such activities. Therefore, when they use these activities, there is often little closure to them and students are left wondering why they are doing what they're doing. This activity encourages the trainee to decide before the class what the objective is and then to devise a communicative activity that matches the goal.

The language in this activity is a bit beyond an ordinary level but not unattainable, and so it shadows a language classroom very well. Much of the vocabulary will be unknown to the trainee-learners, but they will all have some knowledge of the discourse, syntax and grammar. In this activity, trainees can see the struggles their students may encounter in working with such language.

Caveats and Options

1. This activity can also address other issues, such as how to set up a communicative activity, how to structure time limits, how to group students, and how to check their comprehension. The role of the teacher during a communicative activity can also be discussed. Should the teacher be sitting at her desk or facilitating the activity?
2. To expand the linguistic focus of the activity, the teacher can also note language that can be used later to bridge the gap between the activity and further language study. This can help trainees see the differences between the language in the activity and the language they use to accomplish it.
3. Affective issues such as how trainees feel about not showing each other their papers, use of peer correction versus teacher correction, and use of competition in the classroom can also be raised and discussed.
4. Beware of the shrewd trainees who match edges! To avoid this, recut the edges of each strip so they no longer match each other.

References and Further Reading

Sample Paragraphs

Klippel, F. (1987). *Keep talking: Communicative fluency activities for language teaching.* New York: Cambridge University Press.

1. *Canine Seclusion Habitat* (dog house)

The canted precipitation deflector and quadruped ingress/egress aperture are the principal elements of the conventional domestic CSH which is a detached anthropogenic quadrilateral territorial carnivorous-companion-ate-mammal protective module deployed in conjunctions with olfactory/sonic-activated real-time perimeter-intrusion annunciator system procedures. With an optional tension-guidance coupling the CSH amply fits denizen with rotary air-foil interception system, nutrient-uptake reservoir, and porcine-femoral calcium encased protein bar.

2. *Hedonic Affect Icon* (smiling face)

HAI is a closed two-dimensional eidetic schematic pictographic non-cognitive anthropoid psychosomatic-tone representation glyph, connoting self-actualized, subjectively optimal proximate-diurnal-segment expectation comprising perimetric oval, elliptic ophthalmic dilation indicia, positive-curvature stomatic arc, and zygomatic flexure.

3. *Hard-Copy Multitask Window Array* (desk)

HMWA is a sedentary-mode ergonomic workstation with the capacity to support gravitational hard-copy file manager, planar processing field, and a random access information manifold. The HMWA is used for interruptive sequential bio-optical scanning, psychomotor-actuated text generation and arithmetic operations, featuring visually discriminable nonvolatile off-line storage with prehensile data retrieval, and operator-resident processing protocols for alphanumeric graphic input and outputs. It is used with a task-motivating somatic positioner with contoured ischial platform.

4. *Accreted Crystalline Anthropoid Homologue* (snowman)

ACAH is a solar-recyclable aqueous transitional-state hominid isomorph containing a cranial thermal gasket, carbon ocular surrogates, apical hypo-cotylous proboscoid prosthesis, thoracic segment, pedimental formation, and manual particulated concentrator, assembled as a juvenile peer-bonding mechanism.

Sample paragraphs from *TECH SPEAK* by Edward Tenner. Copyright © 1986 by Edward Tenner. Reprinted by permission of Crown Publishers, Inc.

Helping Teachers to Conduct Action Research in Their Classrooms

Contributor
Amy B. M. Tsui
*University of Hong
Kong, Hong Kong*

Narrative

Alfred is a secondary school English teacher. He is teaching a Form Two remedial class with 19 students. He is required to identify an area in his teaching that he wants to improve. After audiotaping his lesson and reviewing the recording, he finds that he does not give students equal chances to respond. He counts the total number of responses, their distribution, and whether they are voluntary or nominated. There are 70 responses, 15 nominated and 55 voluntary. Two students responded only when nominated. The highest number of responses from one student is 9 and the lowest only 1. Nine students are below the average of 3.6 responses per student.

He feels that because he has a small class of only 19 students—where the normal size is 35–40—he should be able to give each of the students opportunities to speak. His problem, contrary to what most teachers of Chinese students find, is that about half of the students in this class are very active. They fight for a chance to answer questions and he usually lets the eager ones answer the question.

Alfred transcribes 15 minutes of his lesson, examines his data, and reflects on the causes of the problem. Firstly, he often starts with "Who wants to answer the question?", and this excludes those who do not volunteer. Secondly, he does not want to disappoint the volunteers. Thirdly, he wants to save time because it is likely that the volunteers know the answer and he does not have to spend time explaining the answer. Fourthly, he is afraid of silence in the classroom. Calling on those who volunteer guarantees there won't be embarrassing silences. Fifthly, he seldom praises the students even when their answers are correct or very close.

He draws up the following strategies to tackle the problem:

1. Try to remember who has responded and who has not.
2. Try to give the inactive ones the chance to speak but acknowledge the enthusiasm of the volunteers at the same time.
3. Ask more open-ended questions.
4. Avoid competition in class since the winner is likely to be an active student.

He also rearranges the seats so that an inactive student sits next to an active student, to encourage good pair or group work.

Alfred tries these strategies out for a 6-day cycle. He keeps a record of what he does each day of the cycle and reflects on the successes of each lesson. At the end of the try-out period, he audiotapes another lesson with the same class and counts the responses again. The total number of responses is 55 and all of them are voluntary. There is an even distribution ranging from 2 to 4 per student. He transcribes 15 minutes of this lesson and examines how he allocates speaking turns to students and the feedback he gives them. The data shows that he gives a lot more encouraging feedback and he tries to give opportunities to all students to participate.

Procedure

The following procedural guidelines can be distributed to teachers who are doing action research (see Handout 12).

To the teacher:

1. Audio- or videotape a lesson and then review the recording to identify an area you wish to improve. Examples may include how turns are allocated, how to reduce teacher talk and increase student talk, what types of questions are asked, and so on.
2. Transcribe a segment of the lesson, about 15 minutes, that illustrates the area you have identified. Reflect on the causes of the problem.
3. Design strategies for improvement.
4. Write a proposal for action research: What am I going to study? What strategies have I designed to help in this area? How long will I test the strategies? What is my schedule for implementation of the strategies?

5. Try out the strategies and keep a diary of what happens in the class-room.

6. At the end of the try-out period, audio- or videotape another lesson of the same class. Review the recording and see if there are any changes.

7. Transcribe another 15 minutes of the lesson that illustrate the changes that have been made and reflect on the reasons for those changes. Changes can include things that have improved or that have gotten worse.

Rationale

Action research is a very effective way of helping teachers to reflect on their teaching and to come up with their own alternatives to improve their practice. In asking them to record their own lessons, review them, and identify an area for improvement, we are helping them to distance themselves from the lesson and to focus on one problem at a time. Getting teachers to examine the transcript of their own lessons is very valuable because often what they think is happening in their classrooms can be quite different from what is actually going on. In the course of examining their own classroom data, teachers begin to notice problems that they were not aware of before. Providing examples from the transcript to illustrate problems and changes pushes teachers to look for hard evidence to support their claims or intuitions. It is also very useful in taking them beyond merely making impressionistic remarks. Keeping a diary of the try-out period, even when it is very brief, helps teachers to reflect on their own teaching.

Caveats and Options

1. When introducing action research, it is very important to make sure that teachers do not have unrealistic expectations about what they can achieve in a short period of time. When asked to identify an area to work on, teachers tend to come up with long lists of things. It is essential to help the teacher focus on one thing at a time.

2. It is also very important that the focus of action research be feasible, that strategies be devised, and that the changes to be made can actually be observed and measured. For example, a teacher says that his lessons are very boring and he wants to make them more interesting. But unless he has spelled out indicators for what makes

his lesson interesting or boring, it will be very difficult for him to judge whether changes have been made.

3. Asking teachers to develop a proposal together with the transcription, and then discussing the proposal with them, can help to make sure that the proposal is viable and not too ambitious. Teachers will get easily discouraged if they find that they cannot determine whether any change has taken place at the end of the try-out period.

References and Further Reading

Kemmis, S., & McTaggart, R. (Eds.). (1988). *The action research planner* (3rd ed.). Geelong, Australia: Deakin University Press.

Nunan, D. (1989). *Understanding language classrooms: A guide for teacher-initiated action*. Hertfordshire, England: Prentice Hall.

Handout 12

Steps for Doing Action Research in Your Classroom

To the teacher:

1. Audio- or videotape a lesson and then review the recording to identify an area you wish to improve. Examples may include how turns are allocated, how to reduce teacher talk and increase student talk, what types of questions are asked, and so on.
2. Transcribe a segment of the lesson, about 15 minutes, that illustrates the area you have identified. Reflect on the causes of the problem.
3. Design strategies for improvement.
4. Write a proposal for action research: What am I going to study? What strategies have I designed to help in this area? How long will I test the strategies? What is my schedule for implementation of the strategies?
5. Try out the strategies and keep a diary of what happens in the classroom.
6. At the end of the try-out period, audio- or videotape another lesson of the same class. Review the recording and see if there are any changes.
7. Transcribe another 15 minutes of the lesson, which illustrate the changes that have been made, and reflect on the reasons for the change—whether it is positive or negative.

Tsui, A. B. M. (1993). Helping teachers to conduct action research in their classrooms. In D. Freeman, with S. Cornwell (Eds.), *New ways in teacher education.* Alexandria, VA: TESOL.

Team Observation: Making Supervision a Nonthreatening Experience for Teachers

Contributor
Amy B. M. Tsui
University of Hong Kong, Hong Kong

Narrative

The activity proposed here involves a team of three, the supervisor and two teachers on an in-service teacher education program. The two teachers observe each other's lessons together with the supervisor, and the lessons are videotaped. After each team observation, a conference is held to discuss the classroom practices and the thinking behind them. The team members give each other suggestions on courses of action to be taken to address the problems that have been identified. Teachers then review the videotape of their own lessons in the light of the points raised in the conference and make individual plans to implement the suggestions.

The pair of teachers, Mr. Lee and Ms. Yu (pseudonyms), with whom I had used this model are each teaching Form Four in the same school. They both have good relationships with their students but have different teaching styles. Mr. Lee is very informal about classroom procedures. Students do not have to stand up to greet him in unison or raise their hands and wait for his permission to answer questions. The classroom atmosphere is very relaxed. Ms. Yu follows the traditional Chinese classroom procedures. Her students are very quiet and contribute very little. She often has to wait for an answer, which is a source of constant frustration for her.

The two teachers also deal differently with the school's classroom seating arrangement. Ms. Yu uses the classroom as it is arranged in single rows, whereas Mr. Lee asks the students to put the desks together in double rows to facilitate pair work. Ms. Yu's teaching is largely teacher centered, whereas Mr. Lee uses pair work and group work. These differences are

176

immediately apparent in the team observation, and the thinking behind them becomes the focus of discussion in the postobservation conference.

Instead of telling the teachers what they should or should not do, I facilitate the discussion by asking hypothetical questions, such as "If you did this, what do you think would have happened?", sharing my experience with the team and encouraging them to do the same. After the conference, Ms. Yu decides to try out during the following 3 weeks the techniques that Mr. Lee used. In the second team observation, there are very obvious changes in the classroom atmosphere, the interaction mode and the amount her students contribute. The second postobservation conference focuses on how she has brought the changes about and the changes in her perception of teaching.

Procedure

1. Pair up two teachers who teach in the same school or nearby schools. If they teach in nearby schools, it may be necessary to seek permission from the school principals for one to observe the other's lesson during free periods. Arrange observation sessions for both teachers. It is better if the lessons are of a similar nature and level.
2. Have members of the team share their lesson plans before the observation.
3. If possible, arrange to videotape the lessons so that the teachers can review them at home afterwards.
4. Conduct a postobservation conference with both teachers as soon as possible after the observation.
5. At the conclusion of the conference, ask each teacher to agree on a course of action to improve teaching and to carry it out in the following few weeks.
6. Monitor progress from time to time by talking to teachers briefly about what they are doing.
7. Arrange for a second round of team observation and conferencing after 3–4 weeks. Focus on the courses of action taken and whether they are succeeding in achieving the objectives. In discussions, the team agrees on further actions to be taken. Repeat the process as many times as possible or needed.

Rationale

Supervision is a threatening experience for most teachers because they are required to perform in front of their students, and their performance is assessed. The stress is even greater when the supervisor's assessment directly affects whether the teacher receives a professional qualification. As a result, teachers tend to be sensitive to any comments and tend to take proposed alternatives as criticisms. Some get defensive about their teaching, and others try to avoid conflict with their supervisor by doing whatever the latter likes to see. This is an unhealthy situation and undermines the supervision process.

Bringing in another teacher who does not have the role of an assessor can help to redress the balance in the power relationship between the teacher and the supervisor. Questions and comments from the peer are more likely to be taken as different perspectives than as criticisms. The nonthreatening nature of the supervision is enhanced by this reciprocity of the observation. The collaborative nature of the supervision—addressing problems and coming up with solutions as a team—encourages teachers to try out alternatives and to share successful and unsuccessful experiences.

Caveats and Options

1. In pairing, teachers should be allowed to find their own partners because the relationship between them contributes to the success of this activity. They should feel comfortable about sharing their problems and frustrations with each other. This will not work when one teacher feels threatened by the other.
2. In the postobservation conferences, the teacher educator plays a very important role in maximizing the benefit of this activity. One should be very careful not to dominate the discussion but to try to draw out the teachers' ideas and suggestions. In cases where one teacher is obviously more experienced and skilled than the other, be very careful not to make the former into a model or the latter feel inferior.
3. At the end of the postobservation conference, teachers should have a clear idea of what they need to work on and what course of action they are going to take. If the problem is complex and the team needs time to think about the courses of action to be taken, make sure that the team gets together to work out concrete strategies. If there is no agreement on courses of action, there will be a lack of focus for the

next observation, and it will be impossible for all of you to tell whether progress has been made.

References and Further Reading

Freeman, D. (1990). Intervening in practice teaching. In J. C. Richards & D. Nunan (Eds.), *Second language teacher education* (pp. 103–117). New York: Cambridge University Press.

Gebhard, J. (1990). Models of supervision: Choices. In J. C. Richards & D. Nunan (Eds.), *Second language teacher education* (pp. 156–166). New York: Cambridge University Press.

Radio Reading for Teacher Educators

Contributor
Nancy R. Tumposky
Montclair State College,
United States

"Radio Reading" is a classroom technique familiar to teachers of reading, as it is often used in elementary classrooms (see Vacca & Vacca, 1986, 117 ff.).

Narrative

The group of 28 trainees is taking a course titled "Effective Teaching, Productive Learning." They differ in background and in their areas of teacher certification (i.e., history, English, math, French, etc.). We are about to study teacher expectation effects and the power of the self-fulfilling prophecy. Before class, I found a written text (Good & Brophy, 1991), about four pages long, that outlines how expectation effects are formed and communicated, describes Rosenthal and Jacobson's classic (1968) study, *Pygmalion in the Classroom,* and explores the relationship between teachers' beliefs and their classroom behavior. I have copied these four pages, cut them up, and recopied them so that I have four short texts, each one approximately one page long. I number these one through four and make seven copies of each one.

I announce that we will be doing a jigsaw activity, using the four texts. Each group of seven members will study its own text intensively and then will choose one reader to read the section aloud to the whole class. The others in the group will study the text together and will write four questions to ask their classmates. Two questions are to be factual and two, interpretive or inferential. I assign people to groups and allow students to rearrange their chairs; then I pass out the texts. I set a time limit and circulate from group to group, helping when necessary. The students are highly motivated and work well together.

After about 20 minutes, we face our chairs toward the center of the room and begin to present, group by group. First, the reader reads the section aloud and everyone listens. Then, the other members of the group ask their peers the questions they have prepared and evaluate their answers.

I sit on the sidelines and take notes to be used later in discussion. Each group takes about 15 minutes. After the four presentations, the trainees seem to have a sophisticated understanding of the topic, judging from their answers and comments.

Procedure

1. Choose a text that can be logically subdivided into sections. I suggest four or five divisions for four or five groups. Trainees should be able to read independently; the content of the text may be new or familiar. Prepare the text for classroom use by copying each section so that it fits on one page, numbering the section, and making several copies of it.
2. Decide how you want to divide the class for group work and give each group a text section. Each group will work with a different subdivision of the text.
3. In class, explain the procedure to the class, including time limits. Assign groups and have students rearrange themselves. Hand out the texts and then circulate to clarify questions and to check that the groups are on task.
4. Bring the class back together and ask each group turn to read their passage aloud. The other group members ask questions of their peers.
5. Lead a general discussion on the topic after all the groups have had their turn.

Rationale

I first observed this activity being used with a group of experienced teachers in an in-service workshop on the topic of thinking skills; I was impressed with how well it worked in getting them to listen to each other and in shifting the center of attention from the teacher educator. Because one of my own priorities is to model classrooms that are learner centered and where students regard each other as valid sources of knowledge, I decided to try it out in my own teaching.

The activity encourages an analytical, active approach toward material rather than relying on the teacher educator to explain it in a top-down fashion. The formation of questions in small groups helps the trainees to pick apart the content and uncover aspects that may be ambiguous or problematic as well as those that invite reflection.

Caveats and Options

1. This activity seems to work best with content areas that invite multiple interpretations and lend themselves to discussion. It is unsuited for content that is entirely factual. It may work well with case studies.
2. When using one long text, the teacher educator may need to edit each section so it is self-contained and makes sense on its own. For this reason, the preparation time for this activity can be lengthier than for a more conventional lecture.
3. The teacher educator may want to subdivide the class in a certain way to balance groups; for this task, I usually use 3 x 5 index cards, one per student, color coding them for the various factors, such as gender, language background and proficiency, teaching experience, etc.

References and Further Reading

Good, T. L., & Brophy, J. E. (1991). *Looking in classrooms* (5th ed.). New York: HarperCollins.

Rosenthal, R., & Jacobson, L. (1968). *Pygmalion in the classroom.* New York: Holt, Rinehart & Winston.

Vacca, R. T., & Vacca, J. L. (1986). *Content area reading* (2nd ed.). Boston, MA: Little, Brown.

A Metaphor for Participation

Contributor
Leslie Turpin
*School for
International Training,
United States*

Narrative

I learned this activity many years ago in Thailand from a friend, Eed Cefkin, when we were discussing ways to help teachers understand how their students' associations with material affected their learning. The purpose of this activity is to raise trainees' awareness of how they learn, how they work in a group, and what it means to attend to someone else.

Fifteen trainees are seated in a circle on the floor. I open a paper bag and empty its contents in the center of the circle. Rita comments that it looks like the insides of a vacuum cleaner bag. The objects are all small items that I have randomly selected from my house and office before class. They include a dime, a hair clip, a Lego plastic block, a rubber band, a postcard, a piece of chalk, a leaf, the metal clasp from a dog leash, a swatch of fabric, a spoon, a band-aid, a tea bag, a car key, and other everyday items.

I explain that the activity will be done in two stages. The first stage will be done in complete silence. I explain that I will begin by taking an object. The person to my left will then take an object and connect it with the one that I have just taken. The next person looks at the object just picked, takes another object, and connects it to the sequence. This procedure continues until we have gone around the circle twice.

I start the activity by taking the band-aid and putting it on the floor in front of me. Liz, who is sitting next to me, pauses and then picks up a leaf and puts it on the floor in front of her. Takeo takes a tea bag and places it in front of him. The next, a spoon; the next, a leash clasp. This continues until we all have two objects on the floor in front of us.

I then ask everyone to take a few minutes to imagine why we might have chosen the objects we did. After a few minutes of silence, I ask trainees to go around and explain their choices. This is done in the order that items were picked so the explanations, like the selection, go around twice. I begin, saying, "I took the band-aid because it reminds me that I cut myself this morning." Liz continues with, "I took the leaf because it's thin like the band-aid and when it's on the ground it covers something—like a band-aid." Then Takeo says, "I took the tea bag because it's made of leaves." The explanations continue: "I took the spoon because I would need it to stir my tea"; "The dog leash is made of metal like the spoon, so I took it." After we all have explained our choices, I ask them to discuss the meaning of the activity and its relation to teaching and learning.

Procedure

For this activity, the teacher educator needs several randomly selected small objects, a few more than two per participant.

1. Ask trainees to arrange themselves in a circle on the floor or around a large table and place the objects in the center. Everyone must be able to see all the objects and the object each person has taken.
2. Explain that the activity will be done in two parts, the first silently, and that they will go around the circle twice. One by one, trainees will pick an object from the center that they associate with the object picked by the person just before. After all the items have been picked, ask everyone to explain, in order of objects picked, what connection they saw between their object and the one just preceding it.
3. Begin by picking an object and placing it directly in front of you. Go around the circle taking objects until everyone has two.
4. Ask the trainees to take a moment to imagine why other people might have chosen the objects they did.
5. Going around the circle in order, have people explain their choices.
6. Lead a discussion on the meaning of the activity and its relation to teaching and learning.

Rationale

Depending on how it is followed up, this activity provides a metaphor for trainees to look at how they think, how others think, how much we assume about other people's thinking, and how much our own personal frames of reference affect the way we take in new material. It can also provide a metaphor for how people participate in conversations, building on previous speakers' ideas.

Caveats and Options

1. The discussion can last as long as the circle activity. It is important to allow ample time to discuss the exercise; a ratio of 1:1 or 1:2 (activity:discussion) is appropriate.
2. The general discussion can develop using the following questions:
   - What does it mean to attend to someone else? How much can you understand someone without hearing the reasons behind their actions?

- How does this activity relate to the way people learn in groups? How do ideas build from one person to the next? How much do you need to understand to build on someone else's thoughts?
- What did you learn about yourself and others from this activity? What are different ways that people connect to information?
- How might you do this activity with language students?

Although these questions provide direction for the discussion, I have found that the discussions work best when left open so that trainees search for their own meaning from the activity.

3. Issues of role and gender in group participation can be introduced with the following modifications:
   a. Expand the number of items to at least four per person.
   b. Give the instructions (Step 2) but instead of going in order, tell participants that they may go in any order they want, one person at a time. The idea is that the order of turns unfolds "naturally," without any planning.
   c. Ask for two volunteers, who will not participate in the activity, to record the order in which the turns and objects are taken. In Step 5, in which the participants verbalize why they made their choices, first have the observers refer to their notes and reconstruct the order of the turns. Then have participants explain their choice of object, following this order.
   d. In the follow-up discussion, examine why the turn-taking unfolded as it did; look at issues of power, gender, and role in groups.

References and Further Reading

Tannen, D. (1990). *You just don't understand: Women and men in conversation.* New York: William Morrow.

Ethnography and Teacher Training

Contributor
Nelleke Van Deusen-Scholl
California State University, Chico, United States

Narrative

As part of a course in ESL methods, trainees are asked to compile an in-depth ethnography of a nonnative speaker of English. They are paired with students who are enrolled in the intensive English language institute on campus. The main purpose of their assignment is to understand the acculturation process of a nonnative speaker from their subjects' perspective.

The trainees meet with their ethnography partners for a minimum of 1 hour a week in various locations. Some of them meet on campus, where a small classroom is set aside for them; others prefer to meet at home or share activities together such as a lunch or a walk in the park. One trainee has actually arranged to help a student practice for her driver's test, and nearly all their conversations take place in the car.

At first, both groups feel nervous and a little awkward; using a tape recorder seems to hinder spontaneity in their conversations. However, after just a few meetings they find that they have plenty to talk about; and an hour a week seems barely adequate to cover the issues they have begun to explore. On a regular basis, the class works in groups to tackle problems that have come up and to offer suggestions for heading in new directions with their projects. Toward the end of the semester, the students bring in their field notes and work together to organize their data and outline their ethnographies. The last weeks of the term are devoted to oral presentations of the trainees' projects.

At the conclusion of the project, the trainees' relationships with their partners have changed significantly. Where initially the trainees had voiced concerns about imposing on their partner, they found that the nonnative speakers were very appreciative of the opportunity to use English and to become friends with the U.S. students. Many in the groups formed genuine friendships and continued seeing each other after the project was over.

Procedure

1. Prepare the trainees in issues of intercultural awareness through readings and discussions, cross-cultural awareness games, nonverbal communication, and work groups on personal experiences and perceptions (Gochenour & Janeway, 1993). Introduce ethnography through readings and discussions, sample ethnographies, and discussion of data-gathering techniques
2. Ask trainees to list their preferences regarding schedule, male or female partner, location of meetings, etc. Match trainees with students. The pairs exchange phone numbers, and schedule the initial contact.
3. Have the trainees gather data through audiotaped conversations, informal meetings, and field notes.
4. Schedule classroom follow-up during the project. During this follow-up, discuss data elicitation techniques, share problems, and offer suggestions for new directions in the project. It is important to give the trainees time to organize rough data.
5. Have the trainees report their results by developing a written ethnography. Ask them to analyze transcriptions of audiotapes and field notes to select salient themes and topics, note personal observations and comments, and include feedback from subjects.
6. In class, have each trainee make an oral report that summarizes the ethnography and can include (audio)visuals, tapes, videos, maps, pictures, etc.

Rationale

The main purpose of the assignment is for the trainees, many of whom have little or no previous exposure to other cultures and languages, to gain an in-depth understanding of the process of acculturation of a non-English speaker. By viewing the majority culture through the eyes of the nonnative speaker, trainees become more aware of the problems of adapting to life, learning the English language, and fitting into the social environment.

Caveats and Options

1. The nonnative speakers on campus benefit from one-on-one contacts with native speakers. By the end of the project, their teachers note marked improvement in the students' ability and willingness to participate in classroom discussions.

2. Within the university context, this exercise allowed us to see the English language programs as a resource on campus. Rather than viewing these programs as just a service to nonnative speakers, it is essential that we begin to recognize their value in presenting teacher education programs with multicultural experiences and offering the teachers the opportunity to become researchers as well. As a result of this project, many of the prospective teachers expressed an interest in continuing such ethnographic research in their own classrooms.

3. It is helpful to caution the students periodically about some potential problems. They must beware of creating a "tourist guide" rather than a ethnography. Many of them were fascinated by the food, dress, and traditions of the other cultures and had to be reminded that the main purpose of their assignment was to understand the acculturation process of a nonnative speaker from their subject's perspective.

4. Occasional ethical problems may occur. For example, differences in religion or cultural values and attitudes may lead to misunderstandings between pairs. At times, the U.S. students would get too involved in the international students' personal problems. To avoid this, they were advised to remain objective in such matters, at least for the duration of the project.

5. A variation is to involve the international students simultaneously in a project of their own. Our intention, for example, is to have the ESOL students compile a community history with the assistance of their ethnography partners. This will give both groups equal status as researchers and would provide a more tangible benefit for the ESOL students in terms of their course requirements.

6. The project involves a minimum of 15 hours of contact between the trainees and students outside the classroom. Approximately 4–5 weeks of in-class time are devoted to preparation and follow-up of the trainees' individual projects. Before they start their actual case study, the trainees participate in a series of class discussions and activities on cross-cultural awareness. They also become familiar with the concept of ethnography and the process of data gathering.

References and Further Reading

Boglan, R., & Biklen, S. (1982). *Qualitative research for education: An introduction to theory and methods.* Boston: Allyn & Bacon.

Gochenour, T., & Janeway, A. (1993). Seven concepts in cross-cultural interaction. In T. Gochenour (Ed.), *Beyond experience.* Yarmouth, ME: Intercultural Press.

Teacher Awareness of the Language Learners' Situation

Contributor
Kathryn Z. Weed
California State University, San Bernardino, United States

As teachers knowledgeable, comfortable, and interested in our subject, we may forget what it is like to sit as a student and listen to words we don't understand.

Narrative

To orient trainees to the feeling of not knowing the language of the classroom, I have begun to use French as a second language much more extensively in training sessions. I prepare a lesson similar to ones they have been teaching, but conduct it in French. In French, I tell the class what we will be doing, I review what we have done, or talk to them about something I have seen or read. I speak for at least 2 minutes, long enough for the novelty to wear off. I then stop and ask how the trainees felt, writing their comments on the board and ask what strategies they used to understand me. I write these comments on the board as well. We go over their feelings and strategies, making note of the variations among class members.

I then repeat some of what I have already said, speaking at different volumes, speeds, and standing different distances from trainees. For example, I will alternate speaking loudly, softly, quickly, slowly; I exaggerate; I slur; I stand next to a person; I talk into a person's face; I use various techniques I have seen teachers use when talking to their students. Then I stop and ask which techniques helped them. Again there is a variety of answers. Usually, at this point, those who have had some French identify themselves and comment on what they can understand of the proceedings. Their reactions tend to differ from those who have had no French.

After this discussion I then launch into a lesson, a poem, "Les mains sur la tête" (Lafayette Parish Bilingual Program, 1979).

> Les mains sur la tête,
> Les mains sur les genoux,
> Tapez-les en arrière,
> Voulez-vous?
>
> Touchez le nez,
> Et puis les oreilles,
> Touchez la bouche,
> Et puis les orteils.

As I recite the poem, those who have had a little French usually follow some of the poem. Others begin to get impatient. I repeat the poem three times—a pedagogically sound practice—and then ask for reactions. There is more boredom at this point and I sense a feeling of "When will she stop this nonsense and get on with it?" The next time, however, I repeat the poem with the hand motions. The class begins to wake up. Not everyone becomes interested, however, and this is important because those who have been discouraged are harder to engage in the activity. We repeat the poem; by this time some trainees are saying a few words, many are pointing to the appropriate body parts. Again we stop and discuss the differences in their comprehension and their feelings. I then show a chart of the poem. We repeat it, I produce pictures of the body parts, and volunteers are invited to tape the pictures next to the appropriate word. We then discuss what helped and what hindered them in understanding the lesson.

Procedure

1. Introduce the lesson in a second language, speaking for at least 2 or 3 minutes.
2. Note trainees' feelings on the board. Ask for strategies trainees used in the lesson and write these on the board. Lead a discussion on this information.
3. Repeat Step 1, using different extra- and paralinguistic styles: speaking loudly, slowly, moving closer to the person.
4. Ask for, and discuss, trainees' reactions to these changes.

5. Present the poem verbally, making sure to repeat it several times. End with having trainees try to say the poem themselves. Again collect trainees' reactions and strategies.
6. Introduce the meaning of the poem through gestures or pictures.
7. Conclude the activity with a comprehensive discussion that begins with trainees' feelings and affective reactions and moves on to learning strategies. Keep the focus on the trainees' experiences and not on your "teaching" of the lesson.

Rationale

It is easy to talk about comprehensible input, preproduction, and speech emergence, but I feel that until trainees actually experience dealing with another language, they do not have a clear sense of what their own students may be facing. This small demonstration is an initial awareness activity for teachers. Through it they begin to grasp elements that contribute to learning experiences for their students. They further see how they themselves deal with situations that they do not understand. They also learn various strategies others employ in that same situation.

Caveats and Options

1. This exercise can be very upsetting to some people; in using it, the teacher educator faces some hostility. At conferences, people have sometimes left my presentation; in my classroom or at an in-service session, they do not have this option. Usually these people are in the minority, and the majority of the participants, by the end, recognize what I am trying to do and are able to sway their colleagues. I try to incorporate the hostility into the discussion by acknowledging it and addressing the role it may have in the context of the participant's own classroom. Students can have such feelings and we need to recognize them.
2. While the class is being conducted in the second language, the participants will talk among themselves in English. This should be noted and discussed. It is important that teachers recognize that such discussions can be on task even though they are conducted in the native language. Further, when I question participants, some will answer in English. This also needs to be addressed. The participant has often understood the question and knows the answer, but does not know,

or is not yet comfortable with, answering in the classroom language—in this case, in French.

3. It is important to write down all reactions and to discuss the various strategies people employ. Writing down all reactions, including extremely negative ones, recognizes them as part of the learning process (see Stevick, 1980, pp. 3–15).

References and Further Reading

Lafayette Parish Bilingual Program. (1979). Jeux. In M. Saville-Troike (Ed.), *Classroom practices in ESL and bilingual education*. Washington, DC: TESOL.

Stevick, E. (1980). *Teaching languages: A way and ways*. Rowley, MA: Newbury House.

Using the Web and the Jigsaw in Tandem to Support Exploratory Discussions

Contributors
Jerri Willett and
Margaret Hawkins
*University of
Massachusetts at
Amherst, United States*

Sixteen teacher educators come together in order to get to know one another's work better, explore common interests, and look for ways to talk about and share our ideas.

Narrative

A week before the meeting, we distributed a packet of one-page abstracts that we had assembled from the participants. These abstracts, which were like tickets of admission to the meeting, described each person's current interest or research in teacher education.

On arrival, we divide into four groups. Each group is asked to create a web, using one of four issues as its node. These issues have been identified from the abstracts. They are (a) knowledge base for second-language teacher education; (b) contradictory discourses and resistance; (c) theory/practice continuities and discontinuities; and (d) empowering teachers and learners. Each group's task is to take ideas from the 16 abstracts to create the branches of the web, relating the ideas to the group's core issue—the node of the web. To help with our task, the organizers give us one-sentence summaries of each abstract. We also keep track of the interesting issues, questions, problems, and concerns that arise during the discussion.

The group I am in focuses on the topic of contradictory discourses and resistance. We begin by talking about our own work and how it relates to this topic. The conversation is lively and darts back and forth from concepts to concrete examples from our own experiences. Gradually, a web begins to emerge, using some of the ideas we have generated. As we try to make connections, new branches continue to sprout. One of us notices that our time is running short so we begin to look at the other abstracts. Although we only get halfway through these, it is clear that other ideas can be incorporated and help to redefine the issues in interesting ways (see below).

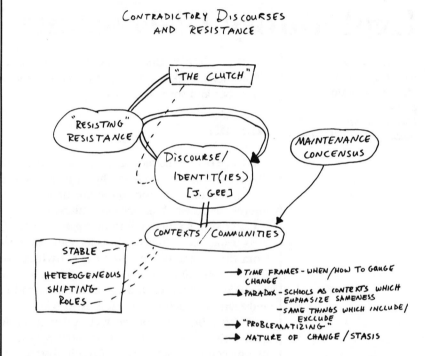

We return to the whole group and listen to the other reports. Although each web looks very different, it seems as if the same excitement has been generated.

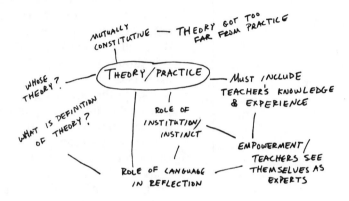

THEORY/PRACTICE CONTINUITIES & DISCONTINUITIES

MUTUALLY CONSTITUTIVE — THEORY GOT TOO FAR FROM PRACTICE

WHOSE THEORY? — THEORY/PRACTICE — MUST INCLUDE TEACHER'S KNOWLEDGE & EXPERIENCE

WHAT IS DEFINITION OF THEORY?

ROLE OF INSTITUTION/ INSTINCT

EMPOWERMENT/ TEACHERS SEE THEMSELVES AS EXPERTS

ROLE OF LANGUAGE IN REFLECTION

TENSIONS: RESISTANCE TO EMPOWERMENT
RELIANCE ON EXPERT VS. CONSTRUCTING
THEORIES & KNOWLEDGE
(NOT A DICHOTOMY!)

The whole group discussion highlights the connections among the four core issues. We feel we are inventing a collaborative language that will help us see our teaching and research in new ways.

Procedure

1. To plan the activity, collect, prepare, and/or assign material that will serve as input for discussion. The material should provide varied points of view on a particular topic. Distribute the materials to participants.
2. Survey the material and select issues or problems that can serve as the node for each web. Each group will tackle the common broad issue from a slightly different perspective.

3. Prior to meeting the group, try out your own web to get a feeling for the possibilities and to prepare yourself to lead a conversation that will connect the group webs.
4. Divide participants into groups and assign topic nodes. Strive for heterogeneity in grouping. Set time limits. We allow 45 minutes for the small-group tasks and 40 minutes for full-group discussion. Provide groups with means to create their webs (i.e., chart paper and markers).
5. Introduce the task and give out the materials. It is important to tell participants not to worry about the kinds of relationships they make nor how they represent these relationships—there are hundreds of different ways to do this.
6. Divide the participants into the assigned groups and begin the discussions.
7. At the end of the time limit, call participants together and have each group display their webs and summarize their discussions. This activity will generate further connections between the webs.

Rationale

The web and jigsaw techniques can be combined to stimulate exploratory discussion, help participants see connections among diverse elements, and encourage equal involvement among the participants. This format, as opposed to isolated presentations, supports an immediate engagement in, and in-depth discussion of, substantive issues and ideas relevant to participants.

The web frees participants from preconceived ordering of the material, thereby helping them to invent new ways of thinking about an issue. The jigsaw ensures that the group recognizes that all participants have something to offer the discussion. Unlike techniques whereby participants are put on the spot to contribute at particular times in particular ways, using these two techniques in tandem encourages a more informal and conversational kind of discussion that puts participants at ease while they take risks.

Caveats and Options

1. It is particularly useful in classes at the end of the course to help trainees integrate concepts they have met throughout the course and apply them to real-life problems. We've used it in both theory and methods classes.

2. Although the two techniques can be used separately, we found that in groups that combine second language speakers with native speakers, the former sometimes have difficulty keeping up with the pace that naturally occurs when the creative juices start flowing. The jigsaw technique helps to make it clear that all participants need to adjust their interaction to include the second language speaker because they need to include his or her information.

3. Working out the timing is very tricky. No matter how much time is allowed, groups never seem to have enough because this is an inherently open activity. It is important to point this out to participants or they may feel disappointed, particularly highly task-oriented learners. Also, it is difficult to tear participants away from their small groups, so be sure to allow enough transition time.

4. It helps to write a description of the task and define the roles that will be needed (i.e., recorder, reporter, facilitator, etc.).

5. If participants need to prepare something beforehand, give them what they need. Our participants prepared abstracts, which they sent us. We then sent a packet to each with all of the abstracts bound together. Participants read these abstracts prior to the meeting.

6. Brainstorming without representing ideas in some way can leave participants with a feeling that the discussion hasn't gone anywhere. The web engenders a sense of having created a product, without closing off other possibilities. The web also helps the group to incorporate and appreciate the diverse ways that participants think about the problem/issue.

7. If the material is selected in such a way that at least some of the connections are easily made, even the most reluctant participant will notice numerous opportunities to enter the discussion. The activity also encourages members to seek out the contributions of all participants.

Telling Herstories:
A Multicultural Diversity
Workshop for Trainees

Contributor

Shelley Wong
*University of Maryland
at College Park, United
States*

Narrative

At my institution, all trainees in the TESOL program, special education, elementary and secondary teaching in all subjects come together once during their semester of student teaching for a day-long multicultural diversity workshop. In past years, the morning session has included one or two keynote speakers usually addressing the teaching of either linguistic or racial minority students or students with special needs. This year we tried a personal approach. Two of us, an Asian American woman and an African American woman, began by telling our family stories.

Bringing photo albums and using an opaque projector, we shared the stories of our families. As an Asian American woman, I shared photos of my paternal grandfather who came from China as a houseboy at age 15 and of the grandmother who was born in a little gold mining town in northern California. I told the story of how the Chinese were burned out when they started to stake claims in the mines; the story of how my American-born grandmother lost her U.S. citizenship by marrying my grandfather because he was from China; how she struggled to get her citizenship back; how she lost a son in World War II; and how the other son returned from the war, went to law school under the GI bill, and later became the first Chinese American judge in the continental United States.

An African American woman, Pamela Higgins Harris included in her presentation an audiotape of the blues, a spiritual, and the themes of pain: the grandfather who told her, "Honey, you don't want to know," when she asked him to tell her about the past. She discussed the theme of color and favoritism—that within the family, her mother, Vivian Shuford Higgins,

From left to right: Earl Wong (grandfather), Delbert Earl Wong (father), Alice Mar Wong (grandmother), Ervin Wong (uncle). Circa 1927.

who was darker skinned, was loved and protected as if to compensate for the contrasting value outside the family. She talked about the values that had been passed on to her, of serving the community, showing a photo of her father, Ashton Higgins, who worked with youth at the Frederick Douglass Community Center in Harlem, New York, for more than 30 years. In the Higgins family, education was highly valued. Her parents were the products of two well-known historically Black colleges in North Carolina: Her mother went to Bennett, her father to A & T (North Carolina Agricultural and Technical College) and earned a doctorate in education at the University of Massachusetts in the 1960s.

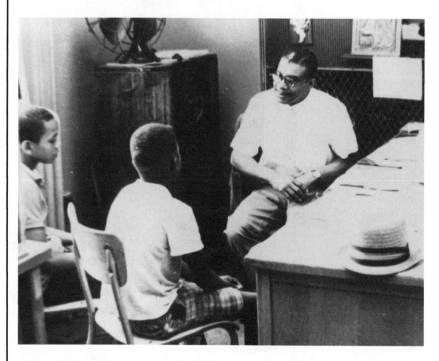

Ashton Higgins, with two boys, at the Frederick Douglass Community Center in Harlem, New York. Circa 1965.

We pointed out that our stories were not "typical" of Asian American or African American families. We didn't want to reinforce the "model minority" stereotype which states that Asian Americans have no problems. Nor did we want family success stories to be interpreted as supporting the Horatio Alger myth that if you "just work hard enough, with education you can make it." This could have led to the corresponding smug implication: "My family made it—why can't they?" At the same time, we wanted to share some of the discrimination that our families had experienced and some of their hardships, triumphs, and contributions to U.S. society. By sharing our family stories, we hoped to create an openness for trainees to talk about and explore the impact of their family backgrounds on their lives and ultimately their teaching.

Procedure

1. Ask the presenter to share stories from her family photo album using an opaque projector for about 15 minutes.
2. From Herstory, ask the trainees to break into small groups to discuss what they found significant.
3. After 10 minutes of small-group work, ask for reactions the participants would like to share with the whole group.
4. Repeat the process (Steps 1–3) with a second Herstory presentation.

Rationale

One of the challenges that Orlando Bravo and Virginia Collier (1985) pose in *Bilingual and ESL Classrooms* is "how ... you get beyond the 'facts, faces and fiestas' approach to multicultural education" (p. 106). Herstories is one answer to that question. It is influenced by bottom-up approaches such as third-world ethnic and feminist studies as well as by theorists like Maxine Greene (1988), who asks what it means to listen for multiple voices in our classrooms.

We cannot listen to the multiple voices in our students without attempting to listen to the multiple voices within ourselves. Herstories begins with our lived history as teachers and educators. The perspective and viewpoint that each of us brings to the classroom is distinct and unique. By being in touch with our own stories, showing the personal triumphs and tragedies of our grandmothers and grandfathers, and sharing the experiences of our families, we can begin to explore what it means to listen for those stories in our students, and we can begin to explore what it means to learn and teach in a multicultural and multilingual world.

Caveats and Options

1. Give each group a few minutes to report back to the whole group.
2. Using these Herstories as an entry point, you can structure discussions in the following way. Have trainees group themselves according to characteristics of racial, religious, economic, family, ethnic origin, or disabilities. Ask each group to discuss the following questions.
   a. In general, what are you most pleased or proud about regarding your group?
   b. What do you most appreciate about members of your group?
   c. What do you least appreciate about members of your group?
   d. How has your group been oppressed or mistreated?
   e. What do some people say or do that reveals their prejudice towards members of your group?
   f. What would you like teachers to know about your group?
   g. What could teachers do to help students who belong to your group?

We thank colleagues Neil Davidson and Richard D. Solomon, who have developed these questions collaboratively working with school districts and teachers on increasing multicultural understanding.

References and Further Reading

Bravo, O., & Collier, V. P. (1985). *Bilingual and ESL classrooms: Teaching in multicultural contexts*. New York: McGraw Hill.

Greene, M. (1988). *The dialectic of freedom*. New York: Teachers College Press.

Also available from TESOL

All Things to All People
Donald N. Flemming, Lucie C. Germer, and Christiane Kelley

A New Decade of Language Testing Research:
Selected Papers from the 1990 Language Testing Research Colloquium
Dan Douglas and Carol Chappelle, Editors

A World of Books:
An Annotated Reading List for ESL/EFL Students
Dorothy S. Brown

Common Threads of Practice:
Teaching English to Children Around the World
Katharine Davies Samway and Denise McKeon, Editors

Coherence in Writing:
Research and Pedagogical Perspectives
Ulla Connor and Ann M. Johns, Editors

Dialogue Journal Writing with Nonnative English Speakers:
A Handbook for Teachers
Joy Kreeft Peyton and Leslee Reed

Dialogue Journal Writing with Nonnative English Speakers:
An Instructional Packet for Teachers and Workshop Leaders
Joy Kreeft Peyton and Jana Staton

Directory of Professional Preparation Programs
in TESOL in the United States, 1992–1994
Helen Kornblum, with Ellen Garshick, Editors

Diversity as Resource:
Redefining Cultural Literacy
Denise E. Murray, Editor

Ending Remediation: Linking ESL
and Content in Higher Education
Sarah Benesch, Editor

New Ways in Teaching Reading
Richard R. Day, Editor

Students and Teachers Writing Together:
Perspectives on Journal Writing
Joy Kreeft Peyton, Editor

Video in Second Language Teaching:
Using, Selecting, and Producing Video for the Classroom
Susan Stempleski and Paul Arcario, Editors

For more information, contact

Teachers of English to Speakers of Other Languages, Inc.
1600 Cameron Street, Suite 300
Alexandria, Virginia 22314 USA
Tel 703-836-0774 • Fax 703-836-7864